NOW THAT'S FUNNY!

NOW THAT'S FUNNY!

Humorous Illustrations to Soup Up Your Talks, Sermons, or Speeches

JACK LORD

RESOURCE *Publications* · Eugene, Oregon

NOW THAT'S FUNNY!
Humorous Illustrations to Soup Up Your Talks, Sermons, or Speeches

Resource Publications
An Imprint of Wipf and Stock Publishers
199 W. 8th Ave., Suite 3
Eugene, OR 97401

www.wipfandstock.com

PAPERBACK ISBN: 978-1-5326-3934-0
HARDCOVER ISBN: 978-1-5326-3935-7
EBOOK ISBN: 978-1-5326-3936-4

Manufactured in the U.S.A.   11/09/17

CONTENTS

INTRODUCTION

WHERE DID I GET THAT JOKE?
From the same place which most of our jokes come; a friend, or the media.

HOW MUCH OF WHAT WE PASS ALONG IN JOKES IS ORIGINAL?
I would guess almost zero.

WHO ORIGINATES THE JOKES?
Who knows? Trying to find the author would be like chasing butterflies in a storm.

I could only name less than five people from whom I have heard anything included here and I doubt that it was original with any of them.

In the event anyone sees something he has originated I apologize for using it without his/her approval.

Meanwhile, here it is,
the best of what I've
heard.

ACCIDENTS

1.

Joe lived in an apartment and had a Grandfather clock. It was a treasure which he had owned for years. One day it stopped working and he wanted to get it to the repair shop before it closed but there was nobody around to help.

After much effort he was able to pick it up and balance it on his back. Then he struggled out the door and down the stairs. Stepping out the front door he wobbled across the lawn. It was impossible to turn his head to see either way as he moved towards his car. A guy who was jogging came dashing over the lawn and ran into him. He hit the ground and the clock fell and broke into a hundred pieces.

Joe shouted.! "With that clock on my back I couldn't see you coming! Why didn't you watch out where you were going?"

"I did! I did! But why don't you wear your clock on your wrist like everybody else?"

2.

Two guys were riding a motorcycle on a cold day. The one in back was freezing and he shouted to the driver, "Stop!" So the driver pulled over.

"I'm freezing back here," he said.

"Well, said the driver, "Turn your jacket around and I'll zip it up the back and the cold air won't come in."

"Good idea," he answered and pulled off his jacket, turned it around and the driver zipped it up.

They climbed back on the motorcycle and went speeding down the road. The passenger hollered, "That's a lot better."

They hadn't gone very far when they rounded a curve, hit a slab of ice, went spinning off the road and hit a tree.

A crowd gathered. Police arrived and finally an ambulance pulled up. The medic ran over to the rookie policeman and asked, "What happened?"

With excitement the policeman answered, "It was horrible, just horrible————When I got here one of them was already dead———————— and by the time I got the other one's head straightened around———- he was dead too!"

3.

ONLY A MAN WOULD ATTEMPT THIS

Last weekend I saw something at Larry's Pistol & Pawn Shop that sparked my interest. The occasion was our 15th anniversary and I was looking for a little something extra for my wife Julie. What I came across was a 100,000-volt, pocket/purse-sized Tazer.

The effects of the Tazer were supposed to be short lived, with no long term adverse affect on your assailant, allowing my wife adequate time to retreat to safety...??

WAY TOO COOL! Long story short, I bought the device and brought it home... I loaded two AAA batteries in the thing and pushed the button. Nothing! I was disappointed. I learned, however, that if I pushed the button and pressed it against a metal surface at the same time, I'd get the blue arc of electricity darting back and forth between the prongs.

AWESOME!!! Unfortunately, I have yet to explain to Julie what that burn spot is on the face of her microwave.

Accidents

Okay, so I was home alone with this new toy, thinking to myself that it couldn't be all that bad with only two AAA batteries, right?

There I sat in my recliner, my cat Gracie looking on intently (trusting little soul) while I was reading the directions and thinking that I really needed to try this thing out on a flesh & blood moving target.

I must admit I thought about zapping Gracie (for a fraction of a second) and then thought better of it. She is such a sweet cat. But, if I was going to give this thing to my wife to protect herself against a mugger, I did want some assurance that it would work as advertised.

So, there I sat in a pair of shorts and a tank top with my reading glasses perched delicately on the bridge of my nose, directions in one hand, and Tazer in another.

The directions said that:

a one-second burst would shock and disorient your assailant; a two-second burst was supposed to cause muscle spasms and a major loss of bodily control; and a three-second burst would purportedly make your assailant flop on the ground like a fish out of water.

Any burst longer than three seconds would be wasting the batteries.

All the while I'm looking at this little device measuring about 5" long, less than 3/4 inch in circumference (loaded with two itsy, bitsy AAA batteries); pretty cute really, and thinking to myself, 'no possible way!'

What happened next is almost beyond description, but I'll do my best.

I'm sitting there alone, reasoning that a one second burst from such a tiny lil ole thing couldn't hurt all that bad. So I decided to give myself a one second burst just for the fun of it.

I touched the prongs to my naked thigh, pushed the button, and...

WOW!!!! WOW!!!!
WEAPONS OF MASS DESTRUCTION!!!!!

I'm sure Hulk Hogan ran in through the side door, picked me up in the recliner, body slammed me on the carpet, over and over and over again. I vaguely recall waking up on my side in the fetal position, with tears in my eyes, body soaking wet, my left arm tucked under my body in the oddest position, and tingling in my legs!

The cat was making meowing sounds I had never heard before, clinging to a picture frame hanging above the fireplace, obviously in an attempt to avoid getting slammed by my body flopping all over the floor.

Note: If you ever feel compelled to test yourself with a Tazer, one note of caution:

There is NO such thing as a one second burst when you zap yourself! You will not let go of that thing until it is dislodged from your hand by a violent thrashing about on the floor! A three second burst would be considered conservative!

A minute or so later (I can't be sure, as time was a relative thing at that point), I collected my wits (what little I had left), sat up and surveyed the landscape.

* My bent reading glasses were on the mantel of the fireplace.
    * The recliner was upside down and about 8 feet or so from where it originally was.
    * My triceps, and right thigh were still twitching.
    * My face felt like it had been shot up with Novocain, and my bottom lip weighed 88 lbs.

* I had no control over the drooling.

* I saw a faint smoke cloud above my head, which I believe came from my hair.

PS: I gave it to my wife and she can't stop laughing about my experience, loved the gift and now regularly threatens me with it!

AIR FORCE

1.

During the war an allied bombing raid had just finished over one of the important targets.. The city had been leveled.

The Red Cross was going from place to place to help survivors. In one area they found a huge house completely demolished but there in the ruins was an old man sitting in a bathtub. They rushed over to help.

As they crowded around to get him out of the tub, he just sat there with a dazed look on his face. "I don't understand it," he muttered. "All I did was pull out the plug."

2.

An air force pilot had trouble with his F-16. Finally, he had to bail out.

As he was dropping, waiting for his chute to open, he looked down and saw an old woman coming up.

He didn't know what to say but, as they sped past one another, he hollered, "Hey, lady, did you see an F-16 going down?"

She hollered back, "No sonny, but did you see a gas stove going up?"

3.

A captain in the air force went into a Japanese café to eat and was visiting with the owner.

"My name is Wilson, what's your name?"

"My name Chow Mein."

"Well, Chow Mein, did you serve in the military?"

"Yes, Chow Mein pilot in air force."

"What kind of plane did you fly."

"Chow Mein fly fighter plane. me Kamakazi pilot"

"Kamakazi pilot? That's strange. I thought Kamakazi pilots crashed their planes into warships on suicide missions.

"Yes, that's right."

"How come you're still alive, Chow Mein?"

"Because me Chicken Chow Mein."

AIRPLANES

1.

The captain of the airline announced as they were flying across country, "Ladies and gentlemen, I'm sorry to announce that one of our engines has just gone out and we are going to be coming into the airport two hours late. But don't worry, we still have three engines left."

About thirty minutes later he announced, "Ladies and gentlemen, I must tell you that we have lost a second engine and this is going to delay our schedule further. We will be an extra three hours landing."

About an hour later he announced, "Ladies and gentlemen. I have another announcement. We have lost our third engine and that is going to delay us another four hours."

One of the lady passengers turned to another and said, "Isn't that just like these airlines. I would guess that if we lose another engine we probably won't get there until tomorrow."

2.

The airplane was flying over the ocean. On the loudspeaker came the voice of the captain. "Ladies and gentlemen this is a recording. The plane has been set on automatic pilot because of trouble in the cockpit.

"The co-pilot and I have ejected and if you will look out your window you will see us in that little rubber raft down below.

"This is part of the emergency system and the airplane will run perfectly well without us. Everything else is in fine working order.

"So just don't worry, everything will be all right,—— be all right,—-
be all right."

3.

Two men were crossing the United States by airline. They left New
York and landed in Chicago. While they were waiting a red fuel
truck came out to gas up the plane.

The plane took off, flew to Denver and landed there. Out
came a red fuel truck and gassed up the plane.

They took off and flew to Reno, landed and a red fuel truck
gassed up the plane.

They took off and were headed for Los Angeles when one
man said to the other, "It's amazing to me how fast these airplanes
can get across the country."

The other answered, "Yeah, but what's more amazing is how
that red fuel truck can make such good time."

ANIMALS

1.

The hunter saw the lion cub and the cub saw the hunter about the same time. The cub decided the hunter would make a good meal and started chasing him right away. The mother lion watched as the young lion chased him around and around a tree.

Finally, she shouted, "Junior, stop that! How often have I told you to stop playing with your food?"

2.

The lion wandered through the jungle. When he saw a tiger, he roared and beat his chest saying, "I'm the king of the jungle." The tiger ducked his tail and ran.

The lion saw a gorilla and roared and beat his chest and said, "I'm the king of the jungle." The gorilla ran for the nearest tree and climbed it.

The lion saw an elephant and roared and beat his chest and said, "I'm the king of the jungle." The elephant reached out with his trunk, grabbed the lion, spun him around his head and threw him against the trunk of a tree.

The lion laid there groggy. Finally, he staggered to his feet, looked over at the elephant and said, "Some people just don't know how to take a joke."

3.

A grocery store had a pet parrot sitting by the check out stand. Customers usually enjoyed it but sometimes it would talk sassy and even use bad words. One day the manager said, "I've told you for the last time to stop talking bad to our customers. If you do it again I'm going to stick you in that freezer over there till you learn better."

The parrot just looked at him and smiled. He talked all right for a few days but then one day he said something ugly to a customer. The manager came over, grabbed him, took him to the freezer, threw him in and slammed the top shut.

About thirty minutes later he went back to the freezer, opened the lid and took out the parrot. It had frost all over its feathers and was so stiff it couldn't move.

"Have you learned your lesson?" asked the manager.

"I did! I did!" said the parrot, "but I just want to ask you one question."

"What is it?"

"I know what I said that put me in that freezer, but what did all of those featherless chickens say that put them in there?"

4.

The lion wandered through the jungle and saw a leopard.

Roaring loudly, he said, "Why aren't you big and strong like I am?" The leopard was scared to death and ran away.

He saw a tiger and roaring he said, "Why aren't you big and strong like I am?" The tiger was scared and ran.

He saw a little mouse and roaring he said, "Why aren't you big and strong like I am."

The little mouse covered his mouth, coughed and answered, "Well, I've been sick."

5.

The pet shop had a parrot that could talk. One day a man came in the front door and, as he passed by, the parrot said, "Hey you!" The man turned around and asked, "Yeah, what do you want?"

The parrot said, "You're the ugliest man I ever saw. In fact, I think you are the ugliest man in the whole world." The man was mad. He went over to the manager and told him, "That parrot over by the door insulted me. I don't know if I want to buy anything here or not."

The manager answered, "I'm sorry, but just leave it to me. I'll take care of him." He went over to the bird and said, "You can't talk like that to our customers. If you talk bad again I'll stick you in that freezer!"

The customer went ahead and shopped. As he left he passed the parrot again. The parrot spoke up, "Hey you!" The man turned around. "Yeah, what do you want?"

The parrot looked back at the manager and then at the customer and said, "Youuuuuu know!"

6.

The Knights in the Middle ages had grown some St. Bernard dogs that were so large they could ride on them. In fact, they always used them to ride on if they had an emergency.

One night it rained real hard while the dogs were outside. An emergency came up and one of the Knights ran to the head Knight and said, "There's an emergency. We better send one of the Knights out on a dog."

"The head Knight answered, "But the dogs are all wet and smelly."

"It doesn't make any difference. We have to send someone out."

"No way," said the Head Knight, "I would never send a Knight out on a dog like this."

7.

A man in the big city used to walk his dog every day. It was a big, mean looking bull dog and whenever someone else was walking their dog they would cross to the other side of the street rather than meet this man and his dog. A few had not done that and the big dog had attacked and beat up their dogs badly. The dog's reputation had grown so everybody knew to avoid him.

One day a new man moved to town and went out walking his little pink dog. Down the street came the other man with his big bull dog. The new man just kept going rather than crossing the street and when they met, the bull dog started a big fight.

But the little pink dog turned around, grabbed the big dog, chewed him up big time and left him lying in a heap.

The bull dog's owner couldn't believe what he saw. He said, "I've never seen anything like that in my life. That's absolutely amazing! He's just a little thing, but he's the strongest dog I ever saw! What do you call him?"

"Well, now we call him Cream Puff," answered the man, "but before we cut off his tail and painted him pink, we called him Alligator."

8.

A man was on the way to the store one day when his car hit a rabbit. He pulled over to the curb and went back to see how bad it was hurt.

It was over by the curb trembling and holding its paw up in the air. He felt sorry for it and looked in his car for something to put on the little rabbit's foot. All he could find was a can of scalp ointment but he went ahead and sprayed it on. Then he put the rabbit over on the grass by the curb and went on to the store.

When he had finished shopping he went back the way he had come to see if the rabbit was still there. He saw it still in the same spot and it seemed to be all right.

In fact, it was just sitting there waving at all the cars going by. The man was amazed.

He decided the scalp spray must have been really good. So he looked to see what kind it was.

On the can were words that read, "Good for damaged hair, and leaves a permanent wave."

9.

THE GREATEST ELEPHANT STORY EVER TOLD
(How to Draw Logical Conclusions)

In 1986, Mkele Mbembe was on holiday in Kenya after graduating from Northwestern University . On a hike through the bush, he came across a young bull elephant standing with one leg raised in the air. The elephant seemed distressed, so Mbembe approached it very carefully.

He got down on one knee and inspected the elephant's foot and found a large piece of wood deeply embedded in it. As carefully and as gently as he could, Mbembe worked the wood out with his hunting knife, after which the elephant gingerly put down its foot.

The elephant turned to face the man, and with a rather curious look on its face, stared at him for several tense moments. Mbembe stood frozen, thinking of nothing else but being trampled. Eventually the elephant trumpeted loudly, turned, and walked away. Mbembe never forgot that elephant or the events of that day.

Twenty years later, Mbembe was walking through the Chicago Zoo with his teenaged son. As they approached the elephant enclosure, one of the creatures turned and walked over to near where Mbembe and his son Tapu were standing.

The large bull elephant stared at Mbembe, lifted its front foot off the ground, then put it down. The elephant did that several times then trumpeted loudly, all the while staring at the man.

Remembering the encounter in 1986, Mbembe couldn't help wondering if this was the same elephant. Mbembe summoned up his courage, climbed over the railing and made his way into the enclosure.

He walked right up to the elephant and stared back in wonder. The elephant trumpeted again, wrapped its trunk around one of Mbembe' s legs and slammed him against the railing, killing him instantly.

And so the logical conclusion from this is that it probably wasn't the same elephant.

10.

There is a very, very tall coconut tree and there are 4 animals, a Lion, a Chimpanzee, a Giraffe, and a Squirrel, who pass by.

They decide to compete to see who is the fastest to get a banana off the tree. Who do you guess will win? Your answer will reflect your personality. So think carefully . . . Try and answer within 30 seconds

Got your answer? Now scroll down to see the analysis. If your answer is:

Lion = you're dull.

Chimpanzee = you're a moron.

Giraffe = you're a complete idiot.

Squirrel = you're just hopelessly stupid.

Because ————————-

A coconut tree doesn't have bananas.

11.

My Favorite Animal – Little boy in class

Our teacher asked us what our favorite animal was, and I said, "Fried chicken." She said I wasn't funny, but she couldn't have been right because everyone else in the class laughed.

My daddy and mama told me to always be truthful and honest, and I am. Fried chicken is my favorite animal. I told my dad what happened, and he said my teacher was probably a member of some animal group that loves animals very much. I do, too, especially chicken, pork and beef. Anyway, my teacher sent me to the principal's office. I told him what happened, and he laughed. Then he told me not to do it again.

The next day in class my teacher asked me what my favorite live animal was. I told her it was chicken. She asked me why, just like she'd asked the other children. So I told her it was because you could make them into fried chicken. She sent me back to the principal's office again. He laughed again and told me not to do it again.

I don't understand. My daddy and momma taught me to be honest, but my teacher doesn't like it when I am.

Today, my teacher asked us to tell her what famous person we admire most. I told her, "Colonel Sanders."

Guess where I am now...???

ARMY

1.

Two guys joined the army and decided to get in the paratroopers.

They were about to jump for the first time and were really scared.

The instructor was trying to reassure them.

"Look," he said, "all you have to do is count to ten and pull the cord and the chute will open but if it fails to open, count to five and pull the emergency cord and the other chute will open Then, when you touch down, the truck will come around and pick all of you up."

They listened carefully but were still scared.

The day came for the jump. They climbed in the plane and the instructor went over the plans again trying to encourage them.——————-but when it came time to jump they were so scared that he had to push them out.

On the way down they counted to ten and each one pulled his cord————- but neither chute opened.———— then they counted to five and pulled the emergency and only one chute opened.

The guy whose chute didn't open hollered as he went by, "That's just like the army ————-nothing works right and they'll probably forget to have the truck pick us up, too!"

2.

The paratrooper was so scared about jumping that every time he thought about it he would stutter.

They kept reassuring him but he would answer, "I j-j-j-just don't know if everything's gonna w-w-w-work."

The day came for the first jump. He was still nervous. The drill instructor told him, "Now don't worry. Just count to ten, pull the cord and everything will be O.K." The private answered, "well, I h-h-h-h-hope so. '

Everybody jumped one by one. The nervous guy was last. He jumped. All the chutes opened and they were floating down when they heard the private whizz by. His chute hadn't opened yet and he was hollering." "f-f-f-f-f-f-f-f-five."

3.

During the war some of the GI's had hired a young
    man to cook for them. They called him Charlie.

He did a good job, but they loved to play practical jokes on him. They would grease the handles on his pots, put water above the door to splash him and a lot of other things.————- They had a great time——————- but he didn't!

One day, as the GI's were talking, they decided that they had been giving him such a rough time that they ought to let up. They sent one of the guys to talk to him. "Charley," he said, "we have been thinking about it and have decided that we have been playing too many tricks on you and we are going to stop it."

Charley looked surprised. He asked, "Are you really going to stop greasing the handles, putting water over the doors and doing all the other things?"

"Yep," said the GI. Charley was really touched and with tears in his eyes he answered, "Well, if you do all that for Charley, then Charley no more spit in the soup."

4.

Johnny was fighting with the Americans against the Germans. They were in the trenches in France and everything was calm.

As he was sitting there, he heard someone from the German side call "Johnny, Johnny." He sat up and listened. He heard it again, "Johnny, Johnny."

Johnny hollered back, "Yeah, what do you want?"

"Where are you?"

Johnny stood up and hollered, "Right here."———————— Bang! He was shot!

They took him back to the hospital area to recover. A few weeks went by and he was talking to one of the other patients. "I still don't know how that guy knew my name."

"That's easy," answered the patient. "He knew that there were a lot of Americans by that name and was just waiting for any one of them to answer."

"Well, I'll be. I never thought of that."

Johnny couldn't wait to get back. He planned to pull a trick on them like they did on him. He knew a lot of them were called Frederick so one day when everything was quiet in the trenches he called out, "Hey, Frederick, Frederick."

"Yeah," came a voice. "Who is that?"

"It's me, Johnny!" he shouted.

"Where are you?"

"Right here," hollered Johnny, as he jumped to his feet.

—————

Bang!!!

BUSINESS

1.

Three kids walked into a grocery store and one of them stepped up to the counter.

The grocer said, "Hello, sonny. what can I do for you?"

"I would like to buy five cents worth of jelly beans," he said.

"All right," said the grocer and he went to the back and brought out a ladder, climbed up to the top shelf and brought down the jellybean box and weighed out five cents worth of jellybeans.

He climbed back up the ladder and put the box on the shelf. Then he climbed down, put the ladder in the back and coming back to the counter handed the bag of jellybeans to the little boy.

"Here you are, son," he said with a smile and, turning to the second boy, he asked, "And what would you like, little man?"

The boy answered, "I would like to have five cents worth of jellybeans."

The grocer stood there a moment looking at him and then headed for the back to get the ladder. He brought the ladder to the front, climbed up to get the box and came down the ladder, weighed out the jellybeans and climbed back up the ladder again with the box.

He placed the box on the shelf and started to go down but stopped. Looking at the third little boy, he asked, "And would you like to have five cents worth of jellybeans, too?"

"No, sir," answered the little boy.

He climbed down the ladder, put it in the back, came back and handed the second little boy his sack.

Then he turned to the third little boy and asked, "Now then, son, what would you like?"

20

The little boy answered, "I would like to have three cents worth of jellybeans."

2.

A man was trying to teach his son the first lesson in business. He put his son on a chair and backed off a step and said, "Now son, jump to papa." The little boy jumped and he caught him.

Then he put him back on the chair and backed off four steps and said, "Now son, jump to papa."

The little boy answered, "But, papa, I'm afraid."

"Just jump," his papa said.

The little boy jumped, but the papa backed away and let the little fellow smack the floor.

The little boy got up crying and sobbed, "But papa, you didn't catch me."

His papa answered, "And that son is your first lesson in business. ————Don't trust nobody, —————-not even your own papa."

3.

A boy said to a man, "Mister, if you'll gimme a nickel my little brother will imitate a chicken."

"What will he do," asked the man, "crow like a rooster?"

"Naw, he wouldn't do anything cheap like that.—————- he'll eat a worm."

4.

A little boy went to the grocery store. The grocer said, "Hello, son, what would you like?"

"Mith-ter, do you have any bird theed?"

"Yes," answered the grocer. "But you're getting big enough to learn how to say it right. Just practice saying bird seed. When you learn you can come back and buy some."

A few days later the boy was back. The grocer said, "Hello again. What would you like?"

"Mith-ter, I want to buy thum bird-theed."

"Not yet, son, not yet. But keep trying."

In a few days he was back. The grocer said with a smile, "Welcome back, sonny, and what would you like?"

"Mith-ter," he said, "Do you know anybody who wanths to buy a dead bird?"

CARPENTERS (Building)

1.

A man was building an outside fireplace and went to the lumber yard to buy some bricks.

He only needed a dozen to finish the job, but the salesman at the yard told him that when he bought a dozen they gave an extra brick. He said that was a nice idea but he didn't need it and they could keep it.

When they put his bricks in the bundle, he paid and left the store. He stopped outside to check what he had and discovered that he had the extra brick.

He was frustrated because he didn't know what to do with it. He went back in the office and told them he didn't want it. They said that he could do whatever he wanted with it. They didn't want it back.

He walked out again, stood around for a while and then simply threw it into the air as far as he could throw it and walked off saying, "I wish all my problems were that easy to get rid of."

2.

A cross country airliner left New York.

They were not fifteen minutes out of the airport when one of the men lit up a cigar. The lady sitting next to him stood it as long as she could and then said, "Sir, if you don't mind, I would appreciate your not smoking. It makes my eyes burn."

He replied, "Lady I bought my ticket for the smoking section and I have my rights and intend to exercise them." and he kept on smoking.

After a while the lady reached under her seat and brought out her cat which had been in a box there. In a few minutes the man began to sneeze.

He turned to her and said, "Lady, please put that cat somewhere else on the plane. I'm allergic to cats."

She answered, "Oh? Well, that's too bad. I enjoy my cat's company."

He kept sneezing and she kept wiping her eyes. Finally, he said, "All right, lady, if you'll get rid of that cat I'll get rid of my cigar."

She agreed and they went to the door of the airplane. He opened the door and she threw out her cat and he threw out his cigar.

They went back to their seats and finished their flight. When they landed in Chicago, she was still grieving about losing her cat.————-

But, as she departed from the plane, she heard a meow and looked over at the wing and saw her cat hanging on to it!

And what do you suppose was in the mouth of the cat????????

No, not a cigar——————————————It was the brick the man threw up in the air!!!!

3.

Two carpenters were working on a roof. One of them missed the nail and began to slip. He kept sliding until he went over the side, but grabbed the edge with the claw on his hammer and struggled to hold on.

While he was sliding, however, he had hit the other one who started sliding and went over the edge, also. The second one grabbed the leg of the first and hung on.

They hollered and hollered for help. Several minutes passed and they were getting tired.

Finally, the first carpenter looked down at the second and said, "Hey, let go of my leg."

The second answered, "Unh, uh."

The first demanded, "I said, let go of my leg."

The other answered, "Unh, uh."

The first one hollered, "If you don't let go of my leg, I'm going to hit you over the head with this hammer!"

4.

Two men were building a house. One of them would pull a nail from his apron, look at it and nail it in——or throw it away. He had a big stack of nails that he had thrown away when the other man came over and asked, "What's this big stack of nails over here for?"

"Oh," he answered, "Those are the ones I've thrown away."

"How come?" He answered, "Because the head's on the wrong end."

"Well, that's dumb," said the other.

"Why?"

"Because they're for the other side of the house."

5.

An Italian came to the United States, became a citizen and was so prosperous that he decided to build a mansion. He hired an architect and construction crew and the work began.

After months of work the architect said that the building was ready and he could come over and inspect it.

The owner was thrilled with what he saw. The architect asked if there was anything else that he could think of that he needed."

"Onlya one thing," he said, "I don'ta see my Halo Statue."

"Your what?"

"My Halo Statue. I wouldn'ta want a house without that."

"I don't understand," said the architect, "What's a Halo Statue?"

"It'sa one of those things that rings and you put it upa by your ear and say, ...'Heylo,—- stat—ue?'"

CHANGING TIMES

1.

The times are changing.————even among the Indians.
The old chief was named Chief Flying Eagle.
His son was called Chief Black Hawk.
And his grandson was named Chief F-22.

2.

A farmer was still enjoying his old Model T. One day he started into town but it broke down. He was standing alongside when a man in a big, new Cadillac pulled up.

"Can I help you?" asked the stranger.

"Well, I don't know what's wrong," answered the farmer.

After looking it over for a while, the man in the Cadillac suggested that they just tie the Model T to the back of the Cadillac and he would pull it to town. The farmer agreed and tied it on. "I'll get in and steer and you go as fast as you want," he said.

"But how will I know if I'm getting too fast?"

"I'll just honk the horn and you can slow down."

"OK," said the man, "Just honk."

They started down the road and picked up speed: forty——fifty—-sixty. The farmer was having a hard time so he blew his horn.

But the man in the Cadillac didn't hear him and just kept speeding up. Now they were going seventy and the farmer laid on his horn.

As they flew by a billboard a policeman was waiting. He stood there a minute or two, then climbed on his motorcycle and pulled out. But he headed in the opposite direction.

He went into town and headed straight for the police station. As he walked in, he took off his gun and badge and laid them on the chief's desk.

"What's this?" asked the chief.

"I'm retiring. Right now!" he answered.

"Why," asked the chief, "What's wrong?"

"Well, times have changed too much. When I see a new Cadillac going down the road at seventy miles an hour and a Model T in back, honking to pass, then I quit."

CHURCH

1.

One of the regular members of the church was having a tough time at home. He was a classic insomniac. Night after night he would lie awake for an hour or so before he could get to sleep.

One night it was especially bad. He tried everything, warm milk, relaxing from head to toe, counting sheep. But nothing worked.

Finally, he dressed, went out to the garage and drove his car down to church. He parked, went into the auditorium, took his usual seat on the back row and fell off to sleep, immediately.

2.

Three boys were playing together.

One of them said, "My dad owns the grocery store and I can get food for nothing." The second said,

"So what? My dad's a doctor and I can get well for nothing."

The last one answered, "Well, listen to this. My dad's a preacher and I can get good for nothing."

3.

A man was being considered for being a deacon. One of the deacons went to interview him. He said, "I am quite pleased with what I have found but before I go I better ask you a Bible question. Let me think. Oh, how about this. Would you please name one of the apostles?"

The man thought a moment and then answered, "Martin Luther."

"What? I'm amazed!" said the deacon, "I didn't think you would know the answer."

4.

What they need is someone to sit at the back of the congregation with a long pole in his hands like they use to do in the old days.

When the service is dull and the sermon is long and tedious and the people are bored, then the man with the pole can reach out over the crowd and tap the preacher on the head and wake him up.

5.

A man at church, without consulting his wife, invited a deacon and his family over for dinner. After they came home the man's wife labored long and hard in the kitchen and finally had everything ready. As they sat down to eat, the dad said to his little girl, "How about your leading us in prayer today?"

She answered, "But I don't know what to say."

"Well," he said, "Just pray like your mother would."

"All right, I'll try," she replied.

She bowed her head and said, "Dear Lord, why in the world did daddy invite these people over here for dinner today?"

6.

The twin boys were identical and so it was very difficult to tell them apart. They grew up in a little town and went off to college.

After the first year they came home and looked for a summer job but couldn't find anything. They were getting desperate when they met the preacher on the street one day. He told them that if they couldn't find anything else they could work as janitors at the church.

They took the job gladly. One day they had all the work done and didn't know what to do. One said, "Let's go up and fix the bell in the tower. It hasn't worked for a long time,"

After a great deal of effort they had it fixed except they couldn't find the clapper to make it ring. They were about to give up when one of them said, "If you'll just pull it to one side and let it go, I'll stand in the middle and let it hit my head."

They tried it and the bell rang beautifully. The other twin tried it too and it worked.

After that, when one of them would meet someone on the street, he would say, "I don't know which one of the twins you are but——- your face sure does ring a bell!"

7.

They were having testimony time at church. One man stood up and said, "I used to run around, drink whiskey, gamble, cuss, and steal but now that I'm a Christian, I've given up almost all of those things."

8.

The pastor was annoyed by one of his members who constantly slept during the sermons.

One day he noticed the man sleeping again and decided to do something about it. He stopped his sermon and said, "Now I want to take a vote. Everyone here who doesn't care a thing about this church, who wishes that the official board was fired and the pastor would quit - -stand up!"

The sleeper woke up with a start. All he heard was,

"Stand up!"

He jumped to his feet, stood for a moment and then, looking around, said,——————— "Pastor, I don't know what we're voting for, but it looks like you and I are the only ones for it."

9.

The pastor was speaking on vision, progress and work for the future. He was trying to stir his church to action.

"We are not going to stand still. This church is going to move!"

"Let it move! Let it move!" answered the congregation.

"This church is not going to just move. This church is going to walk!"

"Let it walk! Let it walk!" they answered.

"This church is going to run so fast it's going to fly!"

"Let it fly! Let it fly!" answered the congregation.

"But if this church is going to fly, it's going to take some money to make it fly!"

The congregation answered, "Let it walk! Let it walk!"

10.

The pastor saw the habitual sleeper in his congregation asleep again. He stopped his sermon and said to the man's wife, "Mrs. Smith, please wake up your husband."

She answered, "You wake him up, pastor. You're the one who put him to sleep."

11.

Maggie was disturbed because her husband always slept in church. She talked to him about it every Sunday after church, but without success.

One day she said to herself, "I'm going to cure him." So when she went to church the next Sunday she took a couple of pieces of garlic in her purse. Her husband hated garlic.

The sermon started and droned along with customary dullness and sure enough the man went sound to sleep.

The lady reached in her purse, pulled out the garlic and, reaching over to her husband, held it under his nose. He shuffled around on his seat and grunted. She left it under his nose and finally, still shuffling with his eyes closed, he said in a loud voice, "Maggie, move your feet, you've got them in my face."

12.

The pastor was preaching on heaven. He told of all the splendid things there.

To climax his message he announced, "Now, folks, we are going to take a vote, "All of you who would like to go to heaven, stand up." Everyone in the congregation stood except one old deacon down front.

The pastor decided that maybe the deacon hadn't heard. So he said a little louder, "Everyone who wants to go to heaven, stand up." Everybody kept standing except the deacon.

The preacher looked over at the deacon and said , "Brother Jones, don't you want to go to heaven when you die?" "Oh, yes," he answered, " I want to go to heaven when I die, but I thought you were getting up a load for right now."

13.

The pastor announced one morning, "After the service this morning, we will have a board meeting down front."

The service was long and the sermon was boring.

After it was over an elderly lady appeared at the front and the pastor said, "Is there anything I can do for you?"

She said, "Well they said they were having a meeting of the board here after church and if anybody was more bored than me, I don't know who it was."

14.

The school teacher said to her class of little children, "I am an atheist and I want to know how many of you are atheists." All of the children, not knowing what an atheist is, raised their hands, except one little girl.

The teacher asked, "Why didn't you raise your hand? What are you?"

"I am a Christian," the little girl replied.

"And why are you a Christian?" asked the teacher.

"Because my Dad is a Christian and my Mom is a Christian and they told me how to be a Christian."

"That's a poor reason," said the teacher. "What if your Dad was a moron and your Mom was a moron, what would you be?"

"Well," she answered, "I would be an atheist schoolteacher."

CRIME

1.

A man sneaked into Mr. Jones watermelon patch late one night. When Mr. Jones heard the dogs barking, he knew what was going on.

He ran out into the back yard with his shotgun pointed to the sky and fired two fast shots.

The man ran out the patch and down the road. But the sheriff caught him and brought him before the judge.

"Where were you when Mr. Jones fired his gun?" asked the judge.

"Which time," asked the man, "the first or the second?

"What difference does it make?" asked the judge.

"About a half a mile," said the man.

2.

This guy wasn't too smart but he was brave. He was held up by a robber one night. The robber said, "Gimme your money or I'll beat you up."

The guy answered, "I'm not gonna do it." The robber beat him up, and then emptied the guy's pockets.

All he found was two quarters and he said , "Hey, stupid, why would you let me beat you to a pulp just to save two quarters?"

"Well, it wasn't because of the two quarters," he answered. "I just didn't want you to take that ten dollar bill I hid in my shoe."

Crime

3.

A big Swede was running from a policeman. He ran around a corner into a clothing store. The owner was his friend so he hollered, "Queek, queek, hide me. There is policeman chasing me."

"Jump into that sack and I'll close it and tell him it's just a sack of bells."

The Swede jumped in. The owner pulled the top together and in rushed the policeman.

"Hey!" he shouted, "Have you seen a big Swede running around here?"

"Can't say that I have."

"Well, what's in that sack over there?"

"Oh that's just a sack of bells."

The policeman said, "Oh yeah?" and walked across the store and gave the sack a big kick.

From inside came the sound, "Yingle, yingle, yingle!"

4.

A man was accused of murdering his girlfriend. They found blood at the scene of the crime and were giving it the DNA test. He was thrown in jail and after a few weeks his lawyer came to visit him with the results.

"I have good news and bad news," the lawyer said. "Which do you want first?"

"Gimme the bad news first, "he answered. "Well, the blood they found at the scene exactly matches your blood." "OK, OK, that's bad all right. But what is the good news?"

"The good news is that your cholesterol is down to 150."

5.

A counterfeiter had made a mistake and printed up a bunch of $18.00 bills. His partner said, "You idiot. Now what are we gonna do? We'll never be able to get these passed."

"Oh, that's no problem," he answered. "I'll just go somewhere way out in the country and get change for them and no one will know the difference."

He drove way out in the country and went in a little store.

The old man at the counter asked, "Hello there young man. Is there something I can do for you?"

"Yeah," he replied, "I need some smaller bills and was wondering if you could give me change for a $18.00 bill?"

"Why sure, be glad to do it," answered the old timer with a twinkle in his eye. "Would you rather have three sixes or two nines?

DEATH (FUNERALS)

1.

After the funeral, the preacher was over at the house of the man who died and was trying to comfort the son.

"Son," he said, "I'm sorry about your dad. I know you're going to miss him. What were your daddy's last words?"

"Daddy didn't have any last words," said the boy. "Momma was with him till he died."

2.

They were having a funeral for a man's wife at the church. But, as the pallbearers were carrying out the casket, they slipped on the step outside and dropped it.

The lid flew open and the lady sat up.

They took her home, she recovered and lived another year.

But then she died and they had another funeral for her.

When the pallbearers were carrying her out, the husband rushed over and said, "Watch out for that step! That's where we had that bad accident last year."

3.

A casket fell out the back of the hearse, rolled down the hill, into a drugstore and banged into the medicine counter.

The lid flew open and the man sat up, looked around, tapped himself on the chest, coughed and asked, "Do you have anything good for this coffin?"

4.

A man was weeping beside a grave at the cemetery. He was there a long time and kept saying, "Oh, if you hadn't died. What a shame. Why did it happen? I wish you were here."

A stranger approached and seeking to be of help, asked, "Was this a relative or a friend?"

"Neither," he answered. "I didn't even know him. But I wish he were back. I really miss him."

"Well, who was he?"

"He was my wife's first husband."

5.

The dad had died and the mother and children were attending the funeral. The pastor was saying nice things about the departed. He kept on and on saying so many good things that finally the mother nudged her boy and whispered, "Johnny, go up and look in the casket and see if that is your daddy."

6.

The preacher had been notified about the funeral at a late date and he was so busy that he had little time to prepare.

He hurried to the funeral home and arrived just before the funeral was to start. The family was already seated so he was ushered to the platform and was waiting to present the sermon when it suddenly dawned on him that he did not remember whether it was a sister or brother who died. He would not know whether to refer to the departed as he or she.

He about panicked. Finally, he motioned to one of the ushers to come to him and he said, "Go check the records and see if it was a sister or a brother who died."

The usher was gone a few minutes and returned just as it was time to speak and whispered, "It was a cousin."

7.

A lady was walking down the street one day when she heard a voice calling, "Sally, Sally."

She stopped and listened but didn't see anyone. As she started walking again, she heard the voice, "Sally, Sally."

She said, "Is someone calling me?"

The voice came again, "Yes, this is your guardian angel. I have good news for you."

"Oh, how wonderful. What is it?"

"I am going to keep the angel of death away from you and you will live to be ninety years old."

"How great! Thank you very much!"

About six months later she was thinking about it and said to herself, "If I'm going to live to be ninety years ago. I might as well fix myself up to look real nice." So she had a face lift, dyed her hair, dieted and lost 50 pounds and bought some new clothes.

About three months later she was hit by a truck and died. As she arrived inside the pearly gates she saw some angels and said, "I want to see my guardian angel."

"There is your guardian angel right over there," one of them said. She walked over and said, "What's the big idea? I thought you told me I was going to live to be ninety years old and I got hit by a truck when I was only 50."

"Oh," the angel answered, "Was that you, Sally? You changed so much I just didn't recognize you."

DOCTORS

1.

A doctor advertised for an office boy to do some general help around the office.

A young man came in and said he would be interested in the job. The doctor told him that he would have to try him out to see if he could do the job. He sent him over to the closet to feed a skeleton a bowl of soup. The young man opened the door, dipped the spoon in the bowl and put the soup to the skeleton's mouth. He didn't know that the doctor was a ventriloquist. Just as he lifted the spoon the doctor threw his voice and from the skeleton came the words, "Tooooo hot!"

The boy threw the spoon in the air, dropped the bowl and ran out the door.

A while later another young man came and asked about the job.

The doctor sent him to the closet as well and, just as he was lifting the spoon, the skeleton said, "Toooooo hot!" The young man left the bowl, the spoon and soup all over the floor just like the first one.

The third young man came in and was told about the skeleton. He was scared but desperately wanted the job. He gritted his teeth and approached the closet. He opened the door, lifted the spoon and then heard the voice, "Tooooo hot!"

He stood frozen, gritted his teeth and said, "Well, blow on it, you bonehead."

2.

Elmer went to the doctor and the doctor asked,

"What is your problem? What can I do for you?"

Elmer answered, "Well, I have this awful pain. Everywhere I touch, it hurts. Watch this." He touched his knee and hollered, "Oh, oh, ohhhhhhh!"

He touched his neck and hollered, "Oh, ohhhhhhhhh!"

The doctor said, "Well, let me look you over. You must have something pretty bad."

The doctor looked and looked. An hour passed. Two hours passed. Finally, after almost giving up, the doctor announced, "I've got it! I've found out what's causing you pain everywhere you touch."

"What is it, what is it?" he asked.

The doctor answered, "You've got a broken finger!"

3.

A man went to see a doctor and said, "Doctor, I have this bad problem. You see (whistle, whistle) every time I start to say something (whistle) I can't get through it without (whistle, whistle) whistling.

"You do have a problem," agreed the doctor. "Let me see if I can help you."

After examining him the doctor said, "I think these pills will be just the thing for you. Take them for two weeks and come back to see me."

"O.K. (whistle, whistle)," said the man, "I'll give them (whistle) a try."

Two weeks later the man was back and the doctor asked, "Did the pills help you?"

The man nodded yes.

"That's great!" said the doctor. "Is there anything else I can do for you?" The man nodded yes. "What is it?" asked the doctor. "Well," answered the man, "I was (snort, snort) wondering if I could (snort, snort) get my whistle back."

4.

As he was walking down the street a man met his doctor.

"I've been wanting to talk to you," the doctor said. "What about?" the man asked.

"Well, I have some bad news and some real bad news for you. Which do you want first." —"Just let me have the bad news first."

"I checked the reports from your exam last week and things are so serious that you only have a week to live."

"Oh, wow, that is bad news! But what can be worse than that?"

"Well, I have been trying to get in touch with you for the last six days!"

5.

There was a lady who was quite a crab, hard to get along with. One day she was feeling very ill and in desperation went to see her doctor.

"I can't imagine what's wrong but I feel terrible." she said. "Sometimes I hurt so much I even foam at the mouth."

The doctor took tests and told her, "I hate to tell you but you are in bad condition; you have hydrophobia.."

"Quick!" she shouted, "Get me some paper and a pen!"

The doctor hurried and brought them to her. "What are you going to do, write out your will?" he asked. "No," she answered, "I'm making a list of the people I'm going to bite!"

DRINKING ALCOHOL

1.

There was a guy who thought it was smart to get drunk every Saturday night. He would go out with other guys and drink and drink. But it would always make him sick.

He would come home and throw up in the kitchen sink and go to bed feeling miserable.

He kept on doing this week after week and his wife kept telling him how terrible that was and how hard on him.

She said, "If you don't quit doing that, one day you're going to throw up all your insides." But he kept on drinking.

One Saturday after he left, his wife was cleaning a chicken for the next day and after taking out all the insides she started to gather them up and throw them away when she thought. "You know, if I left this here and Johnny comes home and throws up, maybe he will think he threw up all his insides and that will make him quit drinking." So she left all the mess in the sink.

Later that night Johnny came home and threw up as usual.

The next morning when he came down to breakfast he said, "Honey I gotta tell you something."

"What is it?" she said sweetly with a twinkle in her eye.

"Well," he said. "I have decided to stop drinking. It turned out just like you said. I came home last night and threw up in the kitchen sink and then I saw that I had thrown up all my insides, —————————-but don't worry, I got the long handle spoon from the drawer and got them all back down again."

DUMB BLONDES

1.

The news is out that two blondes froze to death in a drive-in movie! What happened was they drove into the lot and waited to see the film titled on the sign outside which read, 'Closed for the Winter.'

2.

A blonde was driving home after a game & got caught in a really bad Hailstorm. Her car was covered with dents, so the next day she took it to a repair shop. The shop owner saw that she was a blonde, so he decided to have some fun . . . He told her to go home and blow into the tail pipe really hard, & all the dents would pop out.

So, the blonde went home, got down on her hands & knees & started blowing into her tailpipe. Nothing happened. So she blew a little harder,& still nothing happened.

Her blonde roommate saw her & asked, 'What are you doing?' The first blonde told her how the repairman had instructed her to blow into the tail pipe in order to get all the dents to pop out.

The roommate rolled her eyes & said, 'Hey, Look!
Don't you know you need to roll up the windows first.'

3.

A blonde was shopping at Target & came across a shiny silver Thermos. She was quite fascinated by it, so she picked it up & took It to the clerk to ask what it was.

The clerk said, 'Why, that's a thermos . . .
It keeps hot things hot, And cold things cold.'
'Wow, said the blonde, 'that's amazing....I'm going to buy it!'
So she bought the thermos & took it to work the next day.
Her boss saw it on her desk and asked, 'What's that,'?
'Why, that's a thermos she replied.... It keeps hot things hot &
cold things cold,'.
Her boss inquired, 'Well then, what do you have in it?'
With a big smile she replied.......
'Two popsicles & some hot coffee.'

4.

A blonde goes into work one morning crying her eyes out.
Her boss asks sympathetically, 'What's the matter?'
The blonde replies, 'Early this morning I got a phone call say-
ing that my mother had passed away.'
The boss, feeling sorry for her, says, 'Why don't you go home
for the day? Take the day off to relax & rest.'
'Thanks, she answers but I'd be better off here. I need to keep
my mind off it & I have the best chance of doing that here.'
The boss agrees & allows the blonde to work as usual.
A couple of hours pass & the boss decides to check on the
blonde. He looks out from his office & sees her crying hysterically.
. .
'What's so bad now? Are you gonna be okay?' he asks.
'No!' exclaims the blonde.
'I just received a horrible call from my sister. She said that her
mother died today, too!'

EATING

1.

A man came home from work and was starving, but his wife wasn't home. So he looked in the refrigerator and found some potted meat and fixed himself a sandwich.

When the wife came home she was apologetic about supper not being ready. But he said, "That's all right. I fixed a sandwich with that potted meat."

"What potted meat?" she asked.

"That meat on the second shelf."

"That wasn't potted meat, that was dog food."

"What?????? Dog food?" he said. "Well, it wasn't so bad. In fact, it was pretty good."

After that he made a habit of making a sandwich of dog food every day. His wife told him he better quit it—-it probably wasn't good for him, but he kept doing it.

One day when she was at the doctor's office, she said,

"Oh, by the way, I wanted to ask you something. My husband has been eating dog food every day. Do you think it might hurt him?"

"Yes, indeed," said the doctor. "He better quit that. It might give him ulcers."

She went home and told her husband, but it didn't change a thing. He just kept eating the dog food.

Some months later she went to see the doctor and he asked, "How is your husband?"

She answered, "Oh, I didn't think to tell you. He kept eating that dog food and died last month."

"Oh, I'm sorry," said the doctor. "Did he die from ulcers?"

"No," she answered, "he got run over chasing cars."

2.

A man walked into a cafe.

He asked, "Do you serve crabs here?"

The waiter answered, "We serve anybody. Sit down!"

3.

A man went into a cafe. He ordered steak and vegetables.

It was pretty good and he ate it all.

Then he called the waiter over and asked, "Do you have pie like Ma used to make?"

"Yeah, we sure do," answered the waiter.

"Well, then," he said———"give me some cake."

4.

A man walked into a run down café. Everything was greasy, grimy and dirty but he went ahead and ordered a sandwich. The waiter served him a greasy sandwich and he ate it.

When he was finished, he said, "Gimme some of that raison pie over there."

The waiter answered, "What raison pie over where?"

"Over there," said the man, pointing to the shelf.

The waiter turned, looked at the shelf and then, waving his hand over the pie, he blew hard and said, "That's not raisin pie, that's lemon custard!"

5.

A man from Canada came to visit the United States. He went into a cafe and ordered soup.

He had only taken one bite when he called the waiter over.

"I say, old man, what kind of soup is this?"

The waiter answered, "That's bean soup, sir."

The Canadian answered, "I don't care what's it's bean, what is it now?"

FARMERS

1.

Joe and Oscar had become farmers and were partners. They had new horses and were trying to figure out how they could tell them apart.

"Let's measure how tall they are," suggested Joe.

So they found a measuring tape and measured, but the horses were the same height.

"Let's weight them," said Oscar. So they borrowed some scales and coaxed the horses on. But they weighed exactly the same.

"Let's measure their manes," said Joe. And they did, but they were the same length.

Finally, Oscar said, "Why not measure their tails? That's about our only hope now."

So they measured and found out that one of the tails was two inches longer than the other.

Joe shouted, "Hooray, hooray, we've got the answer. We will always be able to tell them apart! Just remember that the silver horse has a tail two inches longer than the black horse!"

2.

A man was interested in buying a horse from another.

He said, "That's a good looking animal. Is he well trained?"

"Yes," answered the other, "Very well trained. But there's something you need to know. He is a religious horse."

"What does that mean?"

"Well. he is used to getting his commands like this. If I want him to go, I say, 'Praise the Lord,' and if I want him to stop I say 'Amen.'"

"Is that all you have to remember? Just "Praise the Lord " and "Amen?"

"Yep, that's all."

"Well, I'll take him.

The new owner took the horse out to his hill country ranch. He saddled him and mounted up for a ride."

"Giddy up," said the man. but the horse just stood there. He didn't move. "Giddy up" he said again and kicked him in the side. But the horse didn't move. And then the man remembered, "Oh, I mean —Praise the Lord," and the horse took off.

They went a long way. But as they went farther and farther, the horse began to go faster and faster. They were headed for the cliff and the man began hollering, "Whoa, whoa, whoooooaaa" but the horse kept going.

Finally, at the last second, he remembered and shouted, "Amen!"

The horse slid to a stop just inches short of the cliff."

The man sat there looking wide-eyed over at the valley below. He pulled out his handkerchief, wiped the sweat from his brow and exclaimed, "Whew! Praise the Lord."

3.

A farmer had a horse that was so sluggish that he could hardly get him to move. He went to the Vet to see if there was something he could get to help the horse.

"Yes," said the Vet. "We have a new tonic that will make that horse move like he's never moved before. It will really work!"

"Give me some," said the farmer. "That sounds great."

"Be careful how you use it though" cautioned the doctor. "It will make him as wild as can be and you will have a problem catching him and getting him to calm down."

The man eagerly took the bottle back to the farm and waited until the next morning to try it on the horse. He found the horse, gave him the medicine and watched. It worked! It really worked!

The next week the Vet met the farmer on the street and asked about the horse and the new medicine. "It was great, fantastic, wonderful! That must have been powerful stuff because like you said I went out to ride him and he was so excited he wouldn't stop running. It was like he had gone wild."

"Well , did you ever ride him?"

"Yep"

"How did you do it?"

"I finally figured it out. I had to drink the rest of the bottle myself."

4.

A man was going out to see his friend who lived on a farm.

He was driving down the road about thirty miles an hour when he saw a three legged chicken running along beside him.

Pretty soon the chicken ran up and passed him. He sped up to forty but the chicken stayed with him.

Then the chicken went right off and left him.

Way up ahead he saw the chicken turn off. When he got there he noticed it was the driveway of the farmer he was going to see. As he pulled in and climbed out of the car, the farmer came out to meet him.

He said, "Hi, Bill, I want to tell you something. I just saw the strangest thing I've ever seen in my life! There was this three legged chicken and it ran like a deer! I went forty miles an hour and it went right off and left me!"

"Oh, yeah," said the farmer, "that's a special chicken I have been experimenting with to sell to McDonald's. With three legs it ought to really sell!"

"I would think so, but how does it taste?"

"I don't know. I haven't been able to catch one yet!"

5.

The farmer was sick and tired of kids getting in his watermelon patch.

One afternoon he came up with a good idea. He made a sign and put it in the patch that read, "Danger —-one of these watermelons has been poisoned!"

He chuckled as he walked back to the house. That would take care of those thieves.

The next morning he went to his watermelon patch. All the watermelons were there but the sign had been changed.

It read, "Danger—— two of these watermelons have been poisoned!"

6.

A farmer had a good horse but he was sick so he took him to the vet. The vet said, "No question about it. He's sick all right. Here, let me give you some medicine that should take care of it. But there is one big problem. The medicine is very, very bitter and it will be almost impossible to get it down him."

"What'll I do?" asked the farmer.

"Well," said the vet, "take a bunch of newspapers, roll them into a tube and put one end in the horse's mouth. Then pour the medicine in and you get on the other end and blow real hard and it will go down."

"O.K. I'll take care of it," said the farmer and he left with the horse and the medicine.

A few days later the vet saw the farmer in town and the farmer looked like he was about to die. The vet said, "You look terrible! What's the matter?"

The farmer answered, "Well, I feel terrible, too. I did what you told me about the horse. I got some newspaper rolled it into a tube and put one end in the horse's mouth and then I poured that bitter stuff in the other end and put my mouth on it to blow, but the horse blew first!"

7.

A man was traveling out in the country when he came to the place where he wanted to turn off but there was a stream of water flowing across the road. About that time he spotted a farmer nearby and he asked, "Is that water very deep?"

"Nope," answered the farmer, "it ain't deep at all."

"Thanks," said the stranger, "That's all I needed to know."

He climbed back in his car and started across the stream, but, in the middle, the car suddenly went down and disappeared from sight.

The stranger swam to the surface, waded out and stomped over to the farmer. He was mad as could be. He shouted, "Why did you tell me that stream was shallow?"

The farmer looked puzzled. "I don't understand it." He held his hand up to his chest. "My ducks were out there a while ago and it only came up to here on them!"

8.

An Old Farmer's Advice

* A bumble bee is a whole lot faster than a John Deere tractor.

* Forgive your enemies. It messes up their heads.

* Don't corner something that you know is meaner than you.

* When you wallow with pigs, expect to get dirty.

* Most of the stuff people worry about ain't never gonna happen anyway.

* Don't judge folks by their relatives.

* Don't interfere with somethin' that ain't botherin' you none.

* Good judgment comes from experience, and experience comes from bad judgment.

* Lettin' the cat outta the bag is a whole lot easier than puttin' it back in.

FATHERS

1.

The dad was standing in an airport with his baby in his arms. The baby was very fretful and was letting it be known. He cried and cried as the dad walked and jiggled him.

The only change for ten minutes was that the baby sometimes cried louder. Occasionally the man would say soothingly, "Calm down, Johnny. Everything's going to be all right. Patience, patience."

This went on another thirty minutes before the little fellow stopped crying and went to sleep. A man, nearby, who had been watching came over and said, "I just want to commend you for being so patient with little Johnny. You talked so nice to him. You were a fine example."

"You don't understand," he answered. " The baby's name is not Johnny. That's my name."

2.

Why Parents Grow Old Faster

One day the boss wondered why one of his most valued employees was absent but had not phoned in sick. Needing to have an urgent problem with one of the main computers resolved, he dialed the employee's home phone number and was greeted with a child's whisper. ' Hello ? '

'Is your daddy home?' he asked.

'Yes,' whispered the small voice.

May I talk with him?'

The child whispered, ' No .'

Surprised and wanting to talk with an adult, the boss asked, 'Is your Mummy there?' 'Yes.'

'May I talk with her?' Again the small voice whispered, ' No '

Hoping there was somebody with whom he could leave a message, the boss asked, 'Is anybody else there?'

' Yes , ' whispered the child, ' a policeman . '

Wondering what a cop would be doing at his employee's home, the boss asked, 'May I speak with the policeman?'

' No, he's busy , ' whispered the child.

'Busy doing what?'

' Talking to Daddy and Mummy and the Fireman , ' came the whispered answer.

Growing more worried as he heard a loud noise in the background through the earpiece on the phone, the boss asked, 'What is that noise?'

' A helicopter ' answered the whispering voice.

'What is going on there?' demanded the boss, now truly apprehensive. Again, whispering, the child answered,

' The search team just landed a helicopter '

Alarmed, concerned and a little frustrated the boss asked, 'What are they searching for?'

Still whispering, the young voice replied with a giggle...

' They're looking for me cause I'm hiding. '

FIRE

1.

The firemen were at the station one day when someone called and reported a fire at his place. "Come right away!" he hollered and hung up. The firemen grabbed their stuff but didn't know where to go so they just sat waiting for the man to call back.

About ten minutes later the phone rang. It was the same man. "Where are you?" he shouted.

You hung up before you told us how to get there,"

"Well, just come the same way you always do!"

"How's that?"

"In that big red truck!"

FISHING

1.

Not far from a little town was a beautiful lake that many of the people
fished in. Although most people would catch fish occasionally, one man would come back with a boatload every time.

The Game Warden became suspicious and asked him one day, "How is it that you come back with a boatload every day? Nobody else can do that. You aren't doing something illegal are you?"

"Warden," the man answered, "how could you accuse me? If you would like to check it out, just come with me sometime."

"You mean you're asking me to go with you? Well, how about tomorrow?"

"Fine, no problem! Just be down at the dock at 6:00 and we'll go out together."

The Warden was there the next morning and the man had the boat ready. They climbed in and rowed to the middle of the lake where the fisherman dropped anchor.

He reached under the seat and pulled out a stick of dynamite, lit it, threw it out into the water and BOOM! Hundreds of fish floated to the surface and he began to dip them out with his net.

The warden's jaw dropped and his eyes were wide with an unbelieving stare. "I can't believe that you would do something illegal like that right in front of the Game Warden!"

The fisherman didn't say a word. He just reached under the seat, pulled out another stick of dynamite, lit it and threw it on the Warden's lap. "Now," he said, "are you gonna sit there and talk or are you gonna fish?"

2.

Two guys rented a boat and went out fishing. The fish were really biting. They had caught about forty when one said to the other, "I'm out of bait. Do you have any more?"

"No," he answered, "I just ran out, too."

"Well, let's go get some more and get back out here."

"Yeah, let's do it."

They started to row back when one said to the other, "Hey, I just thought of something. We got a problem. How we gonna know where to come to? This is a big lake and they may not be bitin' anywhere else."

"I know what to do," answered the other guy. He pulled out a marker and leaned out over the side of the boat. "Watch this!" and he put a big X on the side of the boat. "Just come back to where the big X is."

"Now that's dumb," said the other guy."

"How come?"

"Because they might not give us the same boat."

FIXING THINGS

1.

AMAZINGLY SIMPLE HOME REMEDIES
(That really work!)

1. AVOID CUTTING YOURSELF WHEN SLICING VEGETA-
BLES BY GETTING SOMEONE ELSE TO HOLD THE VEG-
ETABLES WHILE YOU SLICE.

2. FOR HIGH BLOOD PRESSURE ~ SIMPLY CUT YOURSELF
AND BLEED FOR A FEW MINUTES. THIS WILL REDUCE
THE PRESSURE IN YOUR VEINS.

3. TO PREVENT YOU FROM ROLLING OVER AND GOING
BACK TO SLEEP AFTER YOU HIT THE CUT OFF BUTTON
ON YOUR ALARM CLOCK, PLACE A MOUSE TRAP ON TOP
OF IT.

4. YOU ONLY NEED TWO TOOLS IN LIFE: WD-40 AND
DUCT TAPE.
    IF IT'S SUPPOSE TO MOVE, BUT DOESN'T. USE WD-40.
    IF IT'S NOT SUPPOSE TO MOVE, BUT DOES. USE DUCT
    TAPE.

5. IF YOU CAN'T FIX IT WITH A HAMMER, YOU'VE GOT
AN ELECTRICAL PROBLEM.

FORGETFULNESS

1.

A man was feeling bad and went to the doctor. He asked him to give him a full checkup.

After checking him out the doctor said, "There are all sorts of bad things going around and I'm sorry to tell you that you have two of them."

"Go ahead and tell me," said the man, "That's what I came for."

"First of all, you have some hardening of the arteries that is affecting your memory and it's already gotten pretty bad. Then, second, you have cancer in the beginning stages."

"Boy, that sounds bad," said the patient, "Can the cancer be treated?"

"Yes, I'm happy to say it can, but it will take a little while."

"Well, that's not so bad, Doctor. At least I don't have anything else wrong."

2.

A man went to the doctor. "Doctor," he said, "I have a problem."

"What is it?" he asked.

"Well, I just can't seem to remember anything. I constantly forget."

"That's not so bad. I forget things, too. In fact, everybody forgets things. You don't need to worry about it. How long have you had the problem?"

The man answered, "What problem?"

3.

One wonderful thing about losing your memory when you get older is that you can hide your own Easter Eggs!

And you can do it every week!

4.

Two men were talking. One of them asked, "I heard you ate out last night. Where did you go?"

"Let me think. It was — it was — my memory sure is getting bad. Wait a minute and I can tell you. What's that beautiful flower that smells so wonderful and has thorns on the stem?"

"Sounds like a rose."

"That's it! That's it!" he replied. Then he hollered to his wife in the other room, "Hey, Rose! Where did we eat out last night?"

5.

Three ladies were visiting at one of their homes. They were sitting in the kitchen when one said, "My memory is getting so bad that when I'm at the Mall and go up to shop on the second floor I forget what store I was going to."

"That's nothing," said another. "I can go from the living room to the kitchen to get something from the refrigerator and when I open it I forget what I came there for."

"Well," said the third lady, "Let me knock on wood (and she did). I have problems trying to remember things but I'm not that forgetful. I get along pretty well considering my age. But, wait a minute, did you hear someone knocking at the door?"

6.

My "forgetter" is growing bigger,
But my "rememberer" is broke

Forgetfulness

To you that may seem funny
But, to me, it is no joke
For when I'm 'here' I'm wondering
If I really should be 'there'
And, when I try to think it through,
I haven't got a prayer!
Some times I walk into a room,
And say 'what am I here for?'
I wrack my brain, but all in vain!
A zero, is my score.
At times I put some thing away
Where no one is able to see!
But the person who cannot find it
Is, generally, me!
When shopping I may see someone,
Say 'Hi' and have a chat,
Then, when the person walks away
I think, 'who in the world was that?'
Yes, "my forgetter" is getting bigger
While my "rememberer" is broke,
And it's driving me plumb crazy
But to others it's a joke.

FRIENDS AND ENEMIES

1.

The lack of friendship between Winston Churchill and Lady Astor was ominous. There was no love lost.

She said to him one day, "Sir, if I were your wife, I'd put arsenic in your tea."

Churchill answered, "Lady, if you were my wife, I would drink it."

GOOD ADVICE

1.

* Always keep your words soft and sweet, just in case you have to eat them.

* Drive carefully . . . It's not only cars that can be recalled by their Maker..

* If you lend someone $20 and never see that person again, it was probably worth it..

* Never put both feet in your mouth at the same time, because then you won't have a leg to stand on.

* Since it's the early worm that gets eaten by the bird, sleep late.

* When everything's coming your way, you're in the wrong lane.

* Birthdays are good for you. The more you have, the longer you live.

* You may be only one person in the world, but you may also be the world to one person.

* A truly happy person is one who can enjoy the scenery on a detour.

2.

An Old Farmer's Advice

* A bumble bee is a whole lot faster than a John Deere tractor.
    * Forgive your enemies. It messes up their heads.
    * Don't corner something that you know is meaner than you.

* When you wallow with pigs, expect to get dirty.

* Most of the stuff people worry about ain't never gonna happen anyway.

* Don't judge folks by their relatives.

* Don't interfere with somethin' that ain't botherin' you none.

* Good judgment comes from experience, and experience comes from bad judgment.

* Lettin' the cat outta the bag is a whole lot easier than puttin' it back in.

HUNTING

1.

Two men went bird hunting. One of them had been bragging about his hunting dog and couldn't wait for some action to show how good he was. They were out by the lake when one of them shot a bird that fell way out in the water.

In a flash the dog ran out across the water so fast that he didn't get wet. He grabbed the bird without slowing up and still running on top of the water brought it back to the men.

The other hunter didn't say anything. They shot another bird that fell way out in the lake and again the dog retrieved it running over the water.

Still no comment.

This happened the third time but his friend had nothing to say.

The dog owner, with a big smile on his face, asked, "What do you think about my dog? Didn't you notice something different about him?"

"Yeah," answered the other man. "Apparently he doesn't know how to swim very well."

2.

Two guys were out hunting. As they sat down to rest they saw a flock of geese flying overhead.

One said to the other. "Look at that. They always fly in a V formation and one of the ends of the V is always longer than the other."

"Yeah, I've noticed that."

"You know why that is?"

"No."

"It's because there are more geese on that end."

3.

Two hunters went to the north woods to hunt bear. They arrived at the cabin late at night and planned to hunt early the next morning.

When morning came one of them started fixing breakfast but the other couldn't wait. He said ,"I don't want any breakfast. I just want to go find a bear."

The other one said, "O.K. but I'm gonna go ahead and eat and look for a bear later."

The hunter wasn't out more than five minutes when he saw a bear- and the bear saw him. He leveled his gun as the bear came charging! He fired! But missed!

The bear kept coming fast so he spun around, threw down his gun and started running for the cabin.

When he came close to the cabin he hollered, "Open the door, open the door.!"

The door flew open. The hunter came running in with the bear right behind him. He ran through and out the back , slamming the door and yelled, "Here's your bear, I'll go look for mine."

4.

Two hunters were out in the mountains. One of them was walking near the edge of a cliff when he slipped and went over. He fell to a ledge forty feet down and lay there groaning.

The other hunter saw him go over and rushed to the edge. "Hey, Frank, are you all right?"

"Well, I'm alive but hurt bad."

"I'll let a rope down and see if I can pull you up."

"OK"

He tied a rope to a tree and let it down to Frank. "See if you can pull yourself up."

"OK, I'll try . No, wait! I can't do it. My wrist is sprained."

"Well, tie it under your arms and I'll pull you up."

"I can't do that. I think my arm is broken."

"Well, tie it around your waist," he shouted.

"I can't. I can't. I think my back is broken. But, wait, I'll tell you what I can do. I'll just hold the rope between my teeth and you can pull me up."

"Sounds like that'll work. Tell me when you're ready."

Frank scooted around. Finally, when he was in position, he lifted his head and hollered "OK" and jammed the rope in his mouth.

The hunter began to pull slowly. Inch by inch. Inch by inch. Frank hung on by his teeth. Finally, he came into sight and was almost to the top.

The hunter called out, "How are you doing?"

Frank answered, "OKaaaaaaaaaaaaaaaaaaaaaaaaaaaaaay!"

5.

A guy wanted to become a hunter. He went out on a freezing cold day with another guy. They stayed in a cabin that night and when the sun went down it was bitter cold.

One guy climbed in bed and lay there with his teeth chattering. The other hunter walked in and heard him chattering and asked, "What's the matter?"

"I'm freezing," he answered.

The first guy took a look and saw the other's feet sticking out from under the covers. "Hey, no wonder! Your feet are sticking out. Put them under the covers!"

The other shivered and answered, "You think I'm stupid? I'm not going to put those cold things in bed with me!"

IRRITATION

1.

Two men had an all night wait at the airport when their flight was canceled. It was one o'clock in the morning. They read all the newspapers and magazines around and didn't know what to do with themselves.

One said, "Hey, I know what we can do. Let's play a game. Do you know the difference between irritation, aggravation and frustration?"

"No, I don't," answered the other.

"Well, come on over here and I'll show you." He led him to the phone booth. "Just make up any number and tell me."

The other guy gave him a number and he wrote it down. Then dropping a coin in the phone he dialed it.

The phone rang and rang. Finally, someone answered in a very sleepy voice, "Hello."

"Hello, I'm sorry to wake you up, but I would like to speak to Mr. Witherspoon."

"Who?"

"Mr. Witherspoon."

"Well, there's nobody here by that name."

"Sorry," he said and hung up.

He turned to his friend and said, "Now that's irritation."

They went back and sat down. About two o'clock he motioned to his friend and led him back to the phone. He reached in his pocket, pulled out the slip and dialed the same number.

Again the phone rang and rang. Finally, someone picked it up and asked, "Yeah? What do you want?"

"I'm calling for Witherspoon, Mr. Witherspoon."

An angry voice answered, "Look, this is the same number you called before and there aint no Witherspoon here!" And he slammed the phone down.

The man said to his friend, "Now that's aggravation."

They went back and sat down. It was two hours later, four o'clock, when he said to his friend, "Come on," and they went back to the phone.

"I've shown you irritation, and aggravation. Now watch."

Dropping in the coin he called the same number. Again it rang and rang. At last someone answered, furiously, "All right, all right, now what do you want?"

"Hello," he said, "This is Witherspoon. Have I had any calls?"

Then, turning to his friend, he said, "Now, that's frustration!"

JOKES—TELLING THEM

1.

There were a bunch of older men who sat around telling jokes. They kept repeating them so often that they decided to number them and just call the number.

Someone would call 26 and they would laugh. Someone else would call 314 and they would laugh.

One day as they were sitting around someone called 227 and everyone laughed but one man kept on laughing.

Finally, when he stopped, one of the men asked why did he laugh so much.

"Well," he answered, "I never heard that one before."

2.

Another day, when a number was called, everybody laughed except one man. He didn't even smile.

After everyone stopped laughing, someone asked him, "What's the matter? Why didn't you laugh?"

He answered, "It wasn't funny. Some people just don't know how to tell a joke."

LAWYERS

1.

What's the difference when a lawyer and skunk get run over on the highway?

There are skid marks in front of the skunk.

LOVE AND COURTSHIP

1.

Joe and his girl friend were sitting out on the swing one night. They had been going together for twenty-eight years.

She said, "Joe, there's something I want to ask you."

"What is it?"

"Well, you know we've been going together for twenty eight years."

"Yeah, that's right."

"Well, don't you think it's about time we got married?

"Yeah, I guess so," he answered, "but who would have us?"

2.

A college guy said to his friend, "I wish I could get a steady girlfriend like you have."

"That's not hard," answered his friend, "you just have to say the right things."

"Well, I don't know how. I'm going out with Sally tonight. Give me some words to say."

"Say something like this. I think you're wonderful! Your hair is so beautiful and your face so lovely that when I look at you, time stands still."

"Say it again. Let me see if I can remember it."

He repeated, "I think you're wonderful! Your hair is so beautiful and your face so lovely that when I look at you, time stands still."

"I'll try to remember and I'll say it tonight."

They met the next day and the guy who had gone out with his girlfriend was discouraged. He had a black eye and scratches all over his face.

"What happened to you?" his friend asked. "You look awful."

"Well, I couldn't remember what you said but I tried and she beat me up."

"Well, what did you say?"

"I told her I wanted her to know that she was wonderful, her hair was pretty and she had a face that would stop a clock."

MARRIAGE

1.

"Where have you been?" Joe asked Raymond.

"I've just come back from my wife's funeral," Raymond answered.

"Oh, how sad."

"Yeah, and that was my third wife. The other two died a long time ago."

"Oh, I didn't know that."

"Yeah, my first wife died from eating poison mushrooms."

"That's too bad. How did the second one die?"

"She died the same way. From eating poison mushrooms."

"Well, that's sad. But what a coincidence. They died of the same thing. And how about the third?"

"She died from a blow to the head."

"A blow to the head? How did she get that?"

"She wouldn't eat her mushrooms!"

2.

A man and his wife had four children.

One day someone asked, " What are the names of your children?"

"Eenie, Meanie. Meiny and Elmer."

"Why didn't you call the last one Moe?" asked the stranger.

"Cause we ain't gonna have no moe," he answered.

3.

It was the twenty-fifth wedding anniversary for the couple.

Someone said to the husband who looked like a timid soul, "What a record! But how did you do it? How did you get along so well with your wife?"

"Well, it's easy," he replied quietly. "She always let's me have her own way about things."

4.

The bride and groom had only been married two months when they worked out a plan on how to cut down on expenses and save money.

About two weeks later, he came home from work drenched with sweat and looking completely exhausted. His wife was alarmed.

"What happened to you?" she asked.

He answered, "Well, you remember how we planned to save money? I kept thinking about that and figured another way to save and I tried it out today. Instead of paying the bus fare, I ran home behind it and saved all that money."

She answered, "Well, that's dumb! Really dumb."

"Why is that?" he asked.

"Well," she answered, "Why didn't you run home behind a taxi and save a lot more?"

5.

The lady had outlived four husbands. One day someone asked her about them and what they did for employment.

She said, "Well, the first man I married was a banker. The second was an actor, the third a preacher and the fourth an undertaker."

"What a variety! A banker, an actor, a preacher and an under-taker. How did you happen to choose like that?"

"Well, it was easy. I just figured one for the money, two for the show, three to get ready and four to go."

6.

Henry and his wife were sitting out in the moonlight one night.
He didn't talk much but she did.
"Isn't this a beautiful night?" she asked.
"Yep," he answered.
"Does my hair look pretty in the moonlight?"
"Yep."
"Do you think I have lovely eyes?"
"Yep."
"Oh Henry," she said, "you say the nicest things!"

7.

Someone asked, "Hey, Johnny, how many kids do you have?"
"Me and my wife got three kids," he answered.
"Do you expect to have any more?"
"Absolutely not," he answered.

"Why not?"
"Well, because we read some statistics that said that every fourth child born in the world is Chinese———and me and my wife don't know how to speak Chinese."

8.

A wife said to her husband, "I feel neglected. You never tell me that you love me."
"Well, I told you that when we got married," he answered.
"Yes, but that was twenty years ago. You haven't told me since."
"Well, that should have been good enough. If I ever change my mind I'll let you know."

9.

"Don't you ever go anywhere without your wife?" they asked him.
"Nope," he answered, "I never have and I never will."
"Why is that? Give us a reason."
"Well, it's like this. It's because she is sooooo ugly that I don't want to have to kiss her goodbye."

10.

The husband said to his wife as she was driving down the street,
"Hey, you went right through that stop sign! Didn't you see it?"
"Oh," she answered, flippantly, "When you've seen one, you've seen them all."

11.

The husband and wife were talking.
She was going on and on about one thing and another with scarcely a pause. The husband missed a word and said, "What did you say?"
She answered, "I don't know, I wasn't listening."

12.

They were having their twenty-fifth wedding anniversary and someone asked the husband, "How did you make it this far without a lot of fights?"
"It was because of the agreement we made when we first got married," he answered.
"What was that?"
"Well, we agreed that I would make the decision about all the big things that came along, and she would make the decision about

all the little things and so far, in twenty five years, we've never had any big things come along."

13.

Someone said, "You never know what true happiness is until you get married and then it's too late!"

14.

The two young people were getting married pretty young.

As they stood before the preacher, he said, "And do you give all your earthy goods to her whom you are now taking as your wife?"

He answered, "I do."

One guy who knew him whispered to another, "Well, there goes his bicycle."

15.

One day Adam said to God, "You know that woman you made?"

"Yes," answered God.

"Well, she sure is pretty. Why did you make her so pretty?"

"So that you would love her, Adam."

"Well, let me ask another question. I've noticed something else. Why did you make her smell so nice?"

"So that you would love her, Adam."

"Just one more question. I hate to say it, but why did you make her so dumb?"

"So that she would love you, Adam."

16.

A man and his wife were having terrible trouble getting along with each other. One day he said to her, "You know, I feel that the only friend I have around here is my dog. Everybody needs at least two friends."

She answered, "Well, strange as it may seem, I agree with you and I'm going to do something about it."

And she did! She went out and bought him another dog!

17.

While enjoying an early morning breakfast in a northern Arizona café four elderly ranchers were discussing everything from cattle to horses to weather and how things used to be in the "good ole days."

Finally the conversation moved on to their wives. One rancher turned to the fellow on his right and asked, "Roy, aren't you and your wife celebrating your 50th wedding anniversary soon?"

"Yup, we sure are," Roy replied.

"Well, are you going to do anything special to celebrate?" another man asked.

The old rancher thought for a moment, then replied, "Well, when we had our 25th anniversary I took the missus down to Tucson. For our 50th I'm going down there again and pick her up."

18.

Essay by Rufus

(Introductory note by Rufus.) It is important for men to remember that, as women grow older, it becomes harder for them to maintain the same quality of housekeeping as when they were younger. When you notice this, try not to yell at them since they are oversensitive, and there's nothing worse than an oversensitive woman.)

Good advice for you men.

Let me relate how I handle the situation with my wife, Julie. When I took "early retirement" last year, it became necessary for Julie to get a full-time job since we needed extra income and health benefits. Shortly after she started working, I noticed she was beginning to show her age.

I usually get home from the golf course about the same time she gets home from work. Although she knows how hungry I am, she almost always says she has to rest for half an hour or so before she starts dinner. I don't yell at her. I tell her to take her time and just wake me when she gets dinner on the table. I generally have lunch at the club so eating out in the evening is not desirable. I'm ready for some home cooked grub when I hit that door.

She used to do the dishes as soon as we finished eating. But now it's not unusual for them to sit on the table for several hours after dinner. I try to be ıdiplomatic when reminding her several times that they won't clean themselves. I know she really appreciates this.

Another symptom of aging is complaining. For example she will say that it is difficult for her to find time to pay the monthly bills during her lunch hour. I just smile and offer encouragement by telling her that missing lunch completely now and then wouldn't hurt her any (if you know what I mean). I think tact is one of my strong points.

When doing simple jobs, she seems to think she needs more rest periods like taking a break when she is only half finished mowing the yard. I tell her to fix herself a nice, big, cold glass of freshly squeezed lemonade and just sit for a while. And, as long as she is making one for herself, she may as well make one for me too.

Marriage

I know that I probably look like a saint in the way I support her. Showing this much consideration is not easy. Many men will find it difficult.

Nobody knows better than I do how frustrating women get as they get older. However, guys, if you use a little more patience and are less critical of your aging wife because of this article, I will consider that writing it was well worthwhile.

Signed,
Rufus

EDITOR'S NOTE: Rufus died suddenly on March 27th. The police report says that he was found with a Calloway 50-inch Big Bertha golf club wrapped around his neck.

His wife was arrested and charged with murder; however, the all-woman jury found her Not Guilty, accepting her defense that he was asking for the golf club to wear as his bow-tie.

MUSIC

A man lived in an apartment with a teenager living right above him.

One day the teenager bought a saxophone and started practicing it. Day after day he would come home from work and practice.

The man downstairs could hardly stand it. There were four reasons. In the first place he didn't like a sax. Second, the teenager couldn't play it well. Third, he played it loud. And fourth, he didn't know when to quit. The man told his friends that the sax was driving him nutty.

One night the teenager started early and played and played. When it got to 11:00 PM the man could stand it no longer. He went upstairs and knocked on the door. When the young man opened it the neighbor said, "Young man, if you play that sax any more it'll drive me nutty."

The teenager looked at him in surprise and answered, "But mister, I stopped playing two hours ago!"

NAMES

1.

There was a guy whose name was Jim Skunk. All through his early years he hated his name. He cringed every time someone would call him that.

Year after year he kept saying, "When I get old enough, I'm going to change my name. They're not going to call me Jim Skunk anymore." And the day he was twenty-one he went down to the courthouse, filled out the papers and changed his name. As he was walking out one of his friends saw him and yelled, "Hello, Jim Skunk."

"Don't you call me that !" he yelled back. "That's not my name anymore. I just changed it."

"Well, what do we call you now?"

"Call me by my new name, Fred Skunk."

2.

A little boy threw a neighborhood paper route and came to collect. "Hello, son," said the customer. "What can I do for you?"

"I'm here to collect for the paper." The man dug in his pocket and pulled out the money. "OK, son, he said, "Here's your money. But let me ask you; what's your name?"

"My name is George Washington Brown."

"Well, there," he said, "that's quite a famous name you have."

"It ought to be," said the little boy. "I've been throwing this route for three years."

NAVY

1.

What is a WAC?
That's a lady soldier.

What is a WAVE?
That's a lady sailor.

OK then. What is a WOC?
A WOK is somefin you fow at a wabbit.

2.

A rookie sailor was aboard a battleship when he heard the captain say, "We're just about to the equator."

The rookie said, "Oh boy, that sounds exciting! Will we be able to see it?"

The captain took a second look at the sailor and then answered, "Yeah, yeah, we'll see it."

The rookie said, "Good. I can hardly wait."

Thirty minutes later the captain was looking through his telescope and he called to the sailor who was nearby, "Well, there it is. I see the equator."

The sailor rushed over and said excitedly, "Can I see it too?"

"Sure," said the captain, "look through this," and he handed him the scope.

The sailor shut one eye and looked with his other through the scope. "Where is it?" he asked, "I don't see it."

"Keep looking," answered the captain. Meanwhile he pulled a hair from his own head and stretched it over the end of the scope.

The sailor hollered, "Oh, I see it now! I see it! And I see that camel walking across it too."

3.

The ship was part of the U.S. navy. It was wartime and they were in the south Pacific.

On board was a sailor who had been a professional magician. and also on board another sailor who had brought his pet parrot.

When the sailors had finished their duties and had nothing to do they would often ask the magician to do a trick. But, when he had finished, the parrot would say, "Faker, faker, I know that trick." That made the sailors roar with laughter.

This irritated the magician, but the parrot kept it up and he began to hate the parrot. And the parrot hated the magician.

One day they were in enemy waters and the guys said to the magician, "Come on, give us a trick."

The magician began his trick but, in the middle of it, an enemy sub hit them with a torpedo and the ship sank.

Everyone was grabbing for something to hold on to. The magician grabbed a plank that came floating by. And would you believe it, on the other end sat the parrot.

They looked at each other and immediately turned away without saying a word. They didn't talk all afternoon and through the night.

It was the middle of the next day when the parrot finally turned to the magician and said, "All right, I give up. What did you do with the ship?"

4.

A United States battleship was in the south Pacific. It dropped anchor near a little island. Out from the island came a canoe with four natives in it.

They pulled alongside the battleship and one of the natives stood up and hollered to the sailors leaning on the rail about ten stories up.

"Hello, up there. I want to come aboard."

One of the sailors standing by the rail shouted down, "No, this is a United States battleship and you can't come aboard."

"But I wanna come aboard. Right now!" hollered the native.

"Get lost," shouted the sailor, "You're not coming aboard this ship."

"Just who do you think you are?" asked the native.

"Well, if you wanna know, I'm the second officer in command on this ship,"

"Well," shouted the native, "in the future, speak with more respect. I'm first officer aboard this ship."

OLD AGE

1.

Lose you hair? Try rubbing your scalp with a mixture of alum and persimmon juice. It won't make you grow any new hair but it will shrink your head to fit the hair you have.

2.

An old snake decided he better get some glasses since his sight was so bad.

They fitted him for a pair of contacts since he had no ears to hold up the frames.

The next day another snake said, "Do you like your new glasses?"

"Yeah," he answered. "They are the best thing to happen to me in a long time. In fact, they have completely changed my life."

"In what way?"

"Well, for one thing, I found out that for three years I have been dating a garden hose."

3.

Old age is that time in life when you stoop down to tie your shoe-strings and ask yourself if there is anything else you need to do while you are there.

4.

An older man said to another one day, "I notice that now that I am older there are three things that have happened to me."

"What's that?" asked the other.

"Well, the first thing is that I can't hear as well as I use to. The second is that I can't see as well as I use to. And the third is that, —is that—-hmmm."

5.

They were having a birthday party for a man who was 100 years old.

"How are you getting along," they asked.

He smiled, "Just great, just great. And I ain't got an enemy in the world."

"Is that right?"

"Yep, I outlived them all."

OVERWEIGHT

1.

Overweight? Someone said,
"If you are overweight eat garlic. It won't make you lose weight, but you'll look smaller at a distance."

2.

The fat lady climbed on the scales.
Out came a card which read,
"One at a time please."

PREACHERS

1.

The young preacher finished seminary and went out to preach his first sermon.

He came strutting down the aisle and stepped up on the platform with great pride. When it came time, he tried to preach with impressive eloquence but made a miserable mess.

He left the platform crestfallen and with head hanging low.

Outside the building an elderly lady found him and said, "Sonny, if you had a come in like you went out, you would a went out like you come in."

2.

A preacher started going down to the train station every day. He sat in his car with his watch in his hand and watched as the 3:00 express went by. Then he started his car and went back to church. This continued for months.

Finally, the church board found out about it and they called him in. "We want an explanation," they said.

He answered, "Well I didn't know anybody noticed. But let me put it this way. I go down there for one of the most thrilling moments of my life. I sit there with my watch in hand, waiting for the 3:00 express and when it comes by it's makes my day! It's just wonderful to see something moving and on time, without my having to get behind it and push ."

3.

After the morning service the new preacher was invited for dinner to a deacon's house.

They sat down to eat, had prayer and began to pass the food.

The deacon's son began to giggle. He kept at it for a few minutes until his dad finally asked, "Son, what are you giggling about?"

Catching his breath the boy answered in a big voice, "Look, the new preacher just put some beans on his plate and you and momma said the new preacher didn't know beans."

4.

The visiting preacher explained to the congregation as he started to preach, "I'm just a substitute for the regular preacher and that means that I'm kinda like a cardboard that's put in the window when a pane of glass is broken. It's a substitute for the window pane."

He preached on, long and dry.

The service was finally over and he went outside. A young boy came over and said, "Mister, I want you to know, you weren't a substitute, you were a real pain."

5.

The preacher was preaching on the second coming of Christ. He raised his voice, leaned over the pulpit and shouted the text, "Behold I come."

Further along in the sermon he repeated the text and leaned over the pulpit again shouting, "Behold I come."

Coming to the end of his sermon and, trying for a big finish, he again leaned over the pulpit and shouted, "Behold, I come." but this time he leaned so far that he tumbled over and landed in the lap of an old lady on the front row.

He was red in the face, totally embarrassed. Getting up, he apologized profusely, "I'm sorry, I'm sorry, mam."

But she answered, "That's all right young man, I should have moved. You gave me fair warning three times."

6.

This was the first church for the young seminary graduate to preach in. He was eager to show the benefits of the training he had.

As he began his sermon he announced, "My sermon today is on the story of Noah and I have four points."

"First, Noah and his family before the flood.

Second, Noah and his family during the flood.

Third, Noah and his family after the flood.

And fourth, some miscellaneous thoughts on baptism."

SALESMEN

1.

It was hard times and the insurance salesman was out of a job. He looked everywhere but couldn't find anything. One day he saw an ad in the paper saying they needed help at the zoo. He hustled down there and talked to the head man who told him that their lion had died and they needed someone to dress up in a lion skin and act like a lion until they could get another.

The salesman was desperate so he readily agreed to take the job. He dressed up in the skin, climbed in the cage, shut the door, and went over and laid down. It was a pleasant day and all he did was lie around and go for a walk around the cage occasionally.

After several days he thought this wasn't such a bad job after all. They paid him for just lying around.

He was taking a nap one day when he heard the cage door open and shut. He opened his eyes and looked over to see a lion had been put in the cage with him. He was scared but just sat looking at the lion.

After a while the lion stood up and started moving toward him. He stepped back into the corner and as the lion approached he went for another corner. Pretty soon the other lion was following him around the cage and it became a chase. He was getting tired and started hollering, "Help! Help!"

From in back of him he heard the other lion holler, "Shut up, you idiot, you're not the only salesman out of a job!"

2.

A salesman stopped in a grocery and said , "I was just checking to see if you need any groceries."

"Not now," answered the grocer. "I won't be able to afford anything for a while. I just bought a big supply of salt."

"Well, I noticed you have a lot stacked up there on your shelves."

"You haven't seen anything," said the grocer. "Come back here."

They walked toward the back of the store while the grocer pointed at shelf after shelf stacked to the ceiling with salt boxes.

They went into the back storeroom and it was stacked full of the same.

The grocer led him to the basement and there were more boxes of salt stacked from the floor to the ceiling.

By this time the salesman was absolutely amazed. He said to the grocer, "I've never seen anything like this in all my life. You must be the greatest salt salesman in the world."

"Not me," answered the grocer. "The greatest salt salesman in the world is the guy who sells it to me!"

SCHOOL

1.

The Aggie was excited.

"We are having our class reunion tomorrow! I can hardly wait!"

"Where will it be?" someone asked.

"Back at school, at A&M."

The next day he left. He came back late in the evening and looked dejected.

"What happened?" asked his friend. "Why do you look so sad?"

"Well," he said, "You'd be sad, too, if your school moved and you didn't know where it was anymore."

"What makes you think it moved?" asked the friend.

"Cause, after I drove all those miles down there, I came to a sign on the highway that read, "A&M LEFT.""

2.

He was a college senior but not very bright. He said to another student, "I have an entirely new outlook on life since I took a marriage counseling course."

"Anything in particular you learned?"

"Yeah, for one thing I learned that if your parents never had any children, you probably won't have any either."

3.

Who always borrows?
Never lends?
Your roommate!

Who brings around his low-brow friends?
Your roommate!

Who hogs the only study lamp?
And uses your last postage stamp?
Your roommate!

BUT who is always a friend to you
In spite of all the things you do?
Who knows and loves you through and through?
Your mother.

4.

It was the last day before Christmas vacation and the professor was giving a hard test. One of the guys turned in his paper with a note that read, "Only the Lord knows the answer to these questions. Merry Christmas!" And right beside the note he taped a life saver to the page.

When he returned from vacation he found his test in his mailbox. In place of the life saver was an aspirin along with a note that read, "The Lord gets 100, you get 0. Happy New Year!"

5.

The Texas Aggie had been in school for twelve years and couldn't make grades good enough to graduate. The faculty was getting desperate. They decided to boil it down to one question and graduate him if he could answer it. They planned to ask the question at the end of the regular graduation exercises.

The whole school of 50,000 Aggies gathered at Kyle Stadium. The diplomas were given out and then the President said that they had one last one to give. Up stepped the Aggie and the President said, "If you answer this question correctly you will also graduate. Are you ready?"

"Yep," answered the Aggie.

"From our math department I have this question, How much is six and seven?"

The Aggie thought for a while and then blurted out, "Is it thirteen?"

All 50,000 Aggies in the stands jumped to their feet and shouted, "Give him another chance!"

6.

The absent minded professor came to his science class and announced to the students.

"Now students, the lecture today is on the frog and I have brought a specimen to class with me."

He reached in his desk drawer, pulled out a paper bag, opened it and pulled out a sandwich."

"That's strange," he said, "I distinctly remember having eaten my lunch today."

7.

A man was seated at a banquet one night beside another who appeared to be oriental.

After a while he tried to strike up a conversation, "You like-e food?" he asked.

The oriental, with a questioning look, nodded yes.

Later, as the program was moving along, he turned to him and said, "You like-e program?"

Again the oriental looked at him with a questioning face and nodded yes.

When it came time for the speech the master of ceremonies said, "Ladies and gentlemen, we are privileged to have with us from the university no less than the eminent scholar and head of the English department, Dr. Lee Chow." The man next to him rose to speak and delivered a masterful oration in perfect English.

When he finished he came back to his seat, and, turning to the man who had been questioning him, he asked, "You like-e speech-e?"

8.

School was out and the fifth grader went running across the school ground waving his report card above his head.

"I'm free! I'm free!" he hollered.

A little boy standing over at the side hollered back, "That's nothin, I'm four."

9.

The professor kept missing Johnny in his chemistry class.

After five absences he asked one of the students, "What happened? Johnny has missed the last five classes."

The student said, "Well, Prof, you told us that H_2O was water and H_2SO_4 was sulfuric acid. So let me put it this way:

Johnny was a chemist,
but Johnny ain't no more,
for what he thought was H_2O,
was H_2SO_4."

SPORTS

1.

The high school team was playing against it's arch enemy.

They were having a hard time. Every time one of their players would carry the ball the other team would tackle him so hard that they would have to call time out and take the player out of the game.

But they still hadn't used their star player, Leroy. As the game wore on the team passed a lot instead of trying to run the ball, but they were getting nowhere.

The crowd was getting impatient and began to holler from the stands, "Give the ball to Leroy, give the ball to Leroy."

This kept up for almost five minutes, getting louder and louder. "Give the ball to Leroy, give the ball to Leroy!"

Finally, the quarterback called time out, walked over toward the sidelines and hollered to the crowd,

"Leroy says he don't want the ball."

2.

Two golfers were on the green and one was putting when a funeral went by. He stopped and, taking off his cap, placed it over his heart. When the cars had passed, he replaced his cap and went on with the game.

The other golfer said, "That surprised me, I didn't know you were so sentimental."

"Well," he answered, " I'm not usually, but that funeral was for my wife and today is her birthday."

3.

Martin and Fred grew up playing ball together. Martin was the pitcher and Fred, the catcher. They played on the same team and played almost every day the year round.

One day, Martin, who was the pitcher was told that Fred had been in a big accident and just died. He was dismayed. It took him months to get over it and he didn't enjoy playing ball very much.

One day he was walking down the street when he heard a voice. It sounded like Fred. He said, "That sounds like you, Fred."

"It is Fred. And I'm here in heaven."

"Well, how are you doing?" he asked.

"Wonderful, wonderful. And besides all the other things, I'm the catcher on a good team and get to play ball every day."

"Wow, that sounds great!"

"It is. But let me tell you, I have some good news and bad news. Which would you like first?"

"The good news."

"We are having a game in a couple of hours."

"That's great but what's the bad news?"

"The bad news is you're gonna be the pitcher!"

4.

Four men played golf together for years. One day one of them said to a friend, "I'm kinda bored since our group has stopped playing golf with me."

"I didn't know your group had quit," said the friend. "What happened?"

"Well , it's like this. Do you want to play golf with a liar, a cheat and a thief?"

"No."

"Well," said the golfer, "they didn't want to either."

5.

Fred was an avid golfer. He played every day for years.

But one day he was having a miserable time. Nothing was going right. Finally, on the last green, he missed his putt eight times. He could stand it no longer. He yanked out his clubs , broke them over his knee and threw them in the lake . Then he grabbed the bag and threw it in. He had all the golf he ever wanted.

Storming off the course he headed for the locker room. There he sat with his head on his hands staring down at the floor.

Another golfer came in, saw him and said, "Hey, Fred, we're getting together a foursome tomorrow and need another player. Wanna play?"

Fred jumped to his feet and hollered, "Yeah, what time, what time?"

6.

A golfer was playing when his ball landed on an ant hill.

He was a miserable player and every time he swung he missed the ball and hundreds of ants were killed.

He continued to swing ——and miss. The ants were dying by the thousands. Finally there were only two left and one turned to the other and said, "Well, it looks like the only way we are going to survive is to get on the ball."

7.

He was a big, dumb football player and had played football all evening. It was now midnight when he was walking home.

But he was walking with one foot on the curb and the other in the street, up and down, up and down.

Someone saw him and said, "Hey there, how come you are walking with one foot on the curb and the other in the street?"

"Oh," he answered, "what a relief! I got hurt playing football today and thought I was a cripple for life!"

8.

The Australian was frustrated. He tried and tried for years to throw away his worn out boomerang.

It kept coming back.

9.

A man went out to see his friend in the country and, as he was driving slowly down the road he looked in his rear view mirror and saw a man jogging behind him.

The runner was keeping up with him and he stepped on the gas to get out of the way. But the runner kept coming.

He went fifteen and the runner was still there. He went twenty. The runner was still there. He went twenty five and all of a sudden heard a big explosion.

Looking in the mirror, he saw the runner in a big heap lying in the road. He stopped, backed up, climbed out of the car and ran over to the runner.

"What happened?" he asked.

"Well," he answered, "I was doing real good, and woulda kept up, but my tennis shoe blew out."

10.

There was a near sighted javelin thrower. He could throw the javelin further than he could see and he never knew where it was going.

It never went very far and he didn't break any records, ————but he sure did keep the attention of the crowd.

11.

A little boy was playing ball by himself in his front yard when a man came walking down the street.

"Hey, mister," he said, "You wanta see me hit this ball? I'm the world's greatest batter."

"Sure, son," he answered, "Let me see what you can do."

The little guy threw the ball up and swung the bat. Swish! He missed. He went over and picked up the ball and threw it up again. Swish! Missed again.

"Wait a minute, I'm still the world's greatest batter. Watch this," he called. He picked the ball up and threw it in the air. Swish! He missed again.

"Well, don't get discouraged. Just keep trying," said the man.

"Oh, I'm not discouraged," he said, enthusiastically, "I've decided I'm the world's greatest pitcher!"

12.

The Oklahoma state wrestling championship was being held. The champ who was undefeated was in the finals again. The young man who was challenging him told his coach, "Hey coach, I don't have a chance. This guy won last year and he's undefeated this year."

The coach encouraged him, "Now son, don't give up. You have a good chance. Just one thing you have to keep in mind. Don't let him get you in the pretzel hold. If you do, that's disaster! Watch close and you can keep out of it."

"OK," he answered, "I'll watch out for that pretzel hold."

The wrestlers went out to the mat, the whistle blew and they went at it. They hadn't been going ten seconds when fast as lightning the champ threw the challenger down and locked him in the pretzel hold.

The coach slumped on the bench, covered his face with his hands with his head down. He knew it was all over.

His wrestler was so confused that he didn't know which way was up. But, as he lay there he saw a big toe right in front of his face and he leaned over and bit hard on it.

The coach heard a loud scream and looked up. What he saw amazed him. His wrestler was free from the hold and had thrown the champ down and the referee was counting, "One, two, three!" The match was over.!

The coach ran out and hollered to his wrestler, "That's great. That's great. But how did you do it? I didn't see it."

"Well," answered his wrestler, "I learned something. I didn't know how good I could do until I bit my big toe!"

TEXANS

1.

A Texan was speeding down a California freeway when he was pulled over by a policeman.

The policeman came up to the window and asked, "Why are you driving so fast? What's the big hurry?"

The Texan answered, "I didn't know I was going too fast."

"Where are you going?" he asked.

"I'm going to San Joe-see."

"Where?" asked the officer.

"San Joe-see."

"Would you spell that?"

"That's S-a-n j-o-s-e."

The officer stepped back and laughed and laughed.

When he finally got hold of himself he said, "Out here in California we pronounce our j's like h's. that's San hoe-say. Let me ask, where are you from?"

"Texas"

"How long have you been out here?"

"Well, I came out here in (and he paused)
Hanuary, and I'm goin' back in
Hune or Huly."

2.

A transatlantic airplane was flying over the ocean when the captain announced over the loudspeaker, "We are having engine trouble and are going to have to lighten our load. We must have some volunteers who will jump out of the plane."

The door was opened and an Englishman stepped up and shouted, "God bless the queen," and jumped out the door.

A Frenchman stepped up and hollered, "Viva la France," and jumped out the door.

A Texan stepped up and hollered, "Remember the Alamo," and pushed a Mexican out the door.

3.

A Texas oil man with a big cowboy hat visited Ft. Knox, Kentucky. The guide was showing him around the huge underground gold reserves of the U.S. treasury.

The guide knew the oil man was from Texas so he bragged, "Did you ever see so much gold in your life? We have enough to build a gold fence ten feet high clear around your state of Texas."

"Well," said the Texan, "go ahead and build it and when you're through, if I like it, I'll buy it."

4.

A Texan was visiting Niagara falls. He introduced himself to the guide and told him he was from Texas.

The guide was boasting about the falls. He said, "I'll betcha you've never seen so much water running over a cliff down in Texas."

"No," answered the Texan, "but I know a plumber down there who could fix it in five minutes."

5.

Two rich Texans walked into a Cadillac showroom. They looked at the cars for some time when, finally, one said, "I'll take that one over there."

"Great," said the other, "and I'll take this one here."

One of them reached for his billfold and the other said, "Put it back, put it back, I'll get the bill this. time. You got the hamburgers at the last stop."

6.

A large group of Taliban soldiers were moving down a road when they heard a voice call from behind a sand dune.

"One Texas soldier can whip ten Taliban."

The Taliban commander sent ten of his soldiers over to the dune and a gun battle broke out. After a few minutes there was silence and none of the soldiers returned.

Then a voice from the dune called out, "One Texan can whip fifty Taliban." The Taliban commander was furious. He sent fifty of his best troops over to the dune and instantly there was a huge gunfight. After ten minutes there was silence and none of the fighters returned.

Once more the Texan called out, "One Texan can whip a hundred Taliban."

The commander was absolutely enraged. He picked out a hundred men, armed them with cannons and rockets besides the machine guns and sent them to the dune. A huge battle followed. Then silence.

But finally, one wounded Taliban came crawling over the dune and hollered, "Stop. It's a trap. There are TWO Texans out there."

7.

A furniture salesman traveled the United States selling his product. Often he would be in a new town over the weekend and would attend church.

One day, in a Tennessee church, he noticed a pay phone in the lobby with a sign saying, "Call heaven direct from here for $20." That's interesting, he thought.

Another time he was in a Florida church and saw another phone in the lobby with the sign, "Call heaven direct from here for $20.00."

Just like the other church he noticed. He asked someone why it was so expensive and they told him it was a long distance call. So they charged more.

A few weeks later he was in Texas and there in the lobby was another phone with a sign, "Call heaven direct from here for $1.00."

"I don't get it," he said to an usher. "I saw a phone like that in Tennessee and Florida and they both charged $20.00 for a call to heaven. How come it only costs $1.00 here?"

"Oh," answered the usher, "that's because it's a local call from here."

TEXAS AGGIES

1.

An Aggie saw a tennis player carrying his thermos with him out to the court.

"What's that thing?" he asked.

"Why that's a thermos," said the player.

"What's it for?"

"It's to keep my drinks cold when I put them in cold, or to keep them hot when I put them in hot."

The Aggie looked puzzled, "I don't get it, How does it know?"

2.

Three Aggies went down to the pool for the first summer swim.

As the first one went out on the diving board, he hollered, "Oh boy, I can't wait till Tuesday!" and he jumped.

The second did the same thing. Bouncing on the board he shouted, "Tuesday will be great!" and he jumped.

The third, like the first two, bounced up and down on the board and then hollered as he jumped, "Tuesday will be wonderful."

Across the street one spectator asked another, "Why are all those Aggies so excited about Tuesday?"

"That's the day," he answered, "when they put water in the pool."

3.

An Aggie worked in a factory.

One day, when the whistle blew, everyone grabbed his lunch and went over to eat. The Aggie found a place in the corner and with a happy grin on his face opened his lunch sack. He pulled out a sandwich, unwrapped it and then said, with a big frown, "Oh, noooo, ———peanut butter sandwiches." He ate his lunch gloomily and went back to work.

The next day, the whistle blew, ——- everyone grabbed his lunch and the Aggie headed to his corner. With a gleeful expression on his face. he jerked open his lunch sack, pulled out a sandwich and unwrapped it.

Then he said with a sad look, "Oh, noooo, ———— peanut butter sandwiches."

The next day the whistle blew. Everyone grabbed his lunch and headed over to the corner to watch the Aggie.

With a happy look on his face he tore open his bag, pulled out a sandwich, unwrapped it and again, with disappointment, said, "Oh, noooo, ————peanut butter sandwiches."

Someone said, "Look, if you don't like peanut butter sandwiches, why don't you tell your wife to stop putting them in your lunch?"

The Aggie bristled and answered, "You leave my wife out of this. I fix my own lunches."

4.

An Aggie announced one day to a fellow Aggie that he was going to become a writer.

"I'm gonna write an autobiography," he said.

The other replied, "That's great! That's great! What are you going to write about?"

5.

Do you know why the Aggie took the ruler to bed with him?
He wanted to see how long he slept.

6.

Why did the Aggie take the pitchfork to bed with him?
He wanted to hit the hay.

7.

Why did the Aggie take hay to bed with him?
He wanted to feed his nightmare.

8.

An Aggie was down at the corner one night on his hands and knees.
A friend came up and inquired. "What are you doing?'
"I'm looking for a quarter I lost."
"I'll help you," said the friend and he got down on his hands and knees. They looked for a long time and the friend finally asked, "Where were you when you dropped it?"
"Up there in the middle of the block."
"Well, why aren't we looking up there?"
"Because the light's better down here."

9.

The Aggie said, "When I was little, I swallowed a phonograph needle- but it didn't affect me—affect me——affect me."

10.

An Aggie went to the Post Office to mail a package. He had a hard time getting it in because it was fifty feet long and one inch square.

The clerk said, "We can send it for you but it sure is different. I've never seen a box like this before. Would you mind my asking what's in it?"

"Well, it's like this," said the Aggie, "my neighbor moved away and forgot to take his garden hose so I'm mailing it to him."

11.

"What school did you go to?" they asked the Aggie.

"I went to Texas A&M. And it's about to become the most famous school in the world."

"What makes you say that?"

"Well, you know the Russians were the first to put a man in space and the Americans were the first to put a man on the moon. Now the Aggies are going to be the first to put a man on the sun."

"But they can't do that. It's so hot it would burn him up."

"No problem, we've got that figured out," answered the Aggie. "We're going to put him there at night!"

12.

An Aggie said to another guy, "Hey, guess what I have in this paper bag"

"Aw, I don't know," he answered.

"Oranges, I've got oranges in there. Guess how many and I'll give you one."

"Aw, I can't guess. I don't know."

"Come on and guess. Just gimme a figure."

"I don't know."

"Well, just give it a try. If you guess right, I'll give you both of them."

13.

An Aggie bought a bass boat. He brought it home and his wife looks at him and says, "What you gonna do with that? There ain't no water deep enough to float a boat within 100 miles of here."

He says, "I bought it and I'm a gonna go fishin in it."

His brother, who was an Aggie also, came over to visit several days later. He sees the wife and asks where his brother is. She says, "He's out there in his bass boat," pointing to the field behind the house.

The brother goes out behind the house and sees him sitting in the bass boat way out in the middle of a big corn field with a fishing rod in his hand. He yells out to him, "What are you doing?"

The Aggie in the boat shouts back, "I'm fishin. What does it look like I'm a doing."

His brother yells, "It's people like you that give Aggies a bad name, making everybody think we is stupid. If I could swim, I'd come out there and sink your boat."

14.

A man who just died is delivered to a local mortuary
    wearing an expensive, expertly tailored black suit.
    The aggie mortician asks the deceased's wife how
    she would like the body dressed. She points out that the
    man does look good in the black suit he is already wearing.

The widow, however, says that she always thought her
    H0usband looked his best in blue, and that she wants him in
    a blue suit. She gives the aggie mortician a blank check
    and says, 'I don't care what it costs, but please have my
    husband in a blue suit for the viewing.'

The woman returns the next day for the wake. To her
delight, she finds her husband dressed in a gorgeous blue
suit with a subtle chalk stripe; the suit fits him
perfectly.

She says to the mortician, 'Whatever this cost, I'm very
satisfied. You did an excellent job and I' m very grateful.
How much did you spend?' To her astonishment, the
aggie gives her back the blank check.

'There's no charge,' he says.

'No, really, I must compensate you for the cost of that
exquisite blue suit!' she says.

'Honestly, ma'am,' the aggie says, 'it cost nothing. You
see, a deceased gentleman of about your husband's size was
brought in shortly after you left yesterday, and he was
wearing an attractive blue suit. I asked his wife if she
minded him going to his grave wearing a black suit instead,
and she said it made no difference as long as he looked
nice.'
'So I just switched the heads.'

THRIFTINESS

1.

Do you know why the Scotch don't wear rubber heels on their shoes?

They give too much!

2.

How was the Grand Canyon formed?

By a Scotchman who lost a nickel on the desert.

3.

A Scotch man barely made it to the train station before the train pulled out. He didn't have time to buy a ticket.

They had traveled about a hundred miles when the conductor came through to collect the tickets. The Scotch man explained that he didn't have time to buy a ticket so he would just pay for it now.

He said he was going to Chicago and the conductor told him that it would be $100.00. The Scotchman counted out $80.00 and said that was all he could afford and that should be enough. When the conductor told him that he would have to have twenty dollars more the Scotchman declared he wasn't going to pay any more and there was nothing the conductor could do about it.

"Oh, yes I can," said the conductor, "I can put you off the train."

"You wouldn't dare!" shouted the Scotch man.

ooooooooooooooooo

"Oh, wouldn't I?" shouted the conductor. He reached up and pulled the emergency cord, grabbed the Scotch man's big, heavy suitcase and immediately threw it off the train. When the train stopped, he opened the door and pushed the Scotch man toward the door.

The Scotch man was furious, "I'm going to sue you! I'm going to sue you! You not only make me get off, but you probably killed my son throwing him off."

TRAVEL

1.

A man won the Reader's Digest Sweepstakes and couldn't wait to buy a new car. He picked out the prettiest and fastest he could find and it cost him $500,000.

After taking it out on the road and racing around he came back to town. He stopped at a light and an old man in overalls in an old car next to him leaned over the side and said, "That sure is a pretty car you have there. And I'll bet it goes real fast, too."

"Yeah," answered the man, "just watch this and you'll see." And he took off in a blaze of speed.

He looked in his rear view mirror and there was the old man with his car way back there. But he looked again because the old car was gaining on him and it passed him like a bullet. He didn't know what to think but as he watched he saw the car stop and then it passed him like a bullet going the other way.

He looked again in his mirror and here came the old car back but this time it crashed into a pole right beside him. He jumped out and ran over to the old man and shouted, "Oh, I'm sorry, I'm sorry. Is there anything I can do to help?"

"Yep, you sure can," he answered. "Would you please unhitch my suspenders from your outside mirror?"

2.

Three guys arrived at the train station just as the train was pulling out. They went running down the platform and then jumped down on the tracks after it. One of them barely managed to grab the back end and swung up on the rear. He stood watching and puffing as the other two came.

The train was picking up speed and the next one reached out his hand as the other grabbed it and pulled him up.

But for the last there wasn't a chance. He just stopped and waved to the other two.

He turned around and slowly walked back to the station. A man who had been watching the whole thing said," Well, that wasn't too bad. At least, two out of three of you made it."

"Yeah," he answered, "but the trouble is they came down here to see me off."

3.

Two guys from the country were traveling out west on a train. They had never been away from home and this was all new.

As they were going through the mountains, a man came through the car selling fruit.

What's that long thing there?" asked one.

"Why that's a banana."

"I would like to have one," he said. So he bought it and the other man did too.

He peeled his and took a bite just as the train went through a tunnel. When they came out on the other side, he sat there for a minute then turned to his friend, "Have you taken a bite of that banana?"

"No," he answered.

"Well, don't do it," He said, "It'll make you blind as a bat."

4.

The family was headed out west. They passed the last Filling Station and had gone about five miles into the desert when their car ran out of gas.

The man found a can in the back of the car and went walking the five miles along the blistering hot highway back to the filling station.

He finally arrived at the station. It had a big sign over it reading, "LAST CHANCE FILLING STATION."

As he walked up to the front, he saw the people who ran it sitting outside and he said , "I need to buy some gas."

But one of them answered, "Unh, uh, you can't buy here, you had your chance."

5.

The tourists had not been out on the desert long when their car ran out of water. The man got out, found an empty bottle in the back of his car and started walking back to the last house.

After a long walk he arrived at a little rundown house and knocked. Nobody came to the door so he went around to the back. There in a chair leaning against the back wall in the shade was an old timer.

The man asked, "Do you have some water that I can get a drink and carry some back to the car."

The old man answered, "Yep, right over there," and he pointed to the well.

The tourist went over and drew a bucket of water from the well. Then seeing a dipper he picked it up to get a drink. But he looked back over at the man and saw the long dirty beard with the tobacco juice running down it, so when he started to drink he turned his arm way around backward so he could drink out of the other side of the dipper."

As he was drinking he heard the old man cackling away with laughter.

"What's so funny?" the tourist asked.

"Haw, haw, haw," answered the old man, " you're the only one I ever saw who drank out of a dipper just like me."

6.

The Old Burma Shave Signs——-
    Don't stick your elbow
    Out too far,
    It might go home
    In another car
    Her chariot,
    Raced at eighty per.
    They hauled away,
    What had Ben Hur.

7.

The salesman on the train told the conductor that he was going to be on the train overnight and would be sleeping in the Pullman car.

He explained that he was headed for Cypress Springs for a big meeting that would make a lot of money for him. He asked the conductor to get him up and off the train the next morning at 6:30 when the train would be stopping there The conductor agreed.

Later in the evening, before turning in, the salesman went looking for the conductor. He found him and said. "I just wanted to remind you. I'll be sleeping in next to the last bunk in the Pullman car. I am a hard person to get up in the morning so don't take any excuses. Just get me up and off at 6:30."

"Don't worry," answered the conductor, "I know where you're sleeping. I do this all the time. I'll get you up."

The man went to bed and had a good night's sleep. The next morning he woke up and looked at his watch. It was 7:00! He jumped out of bed, went running through the cars, found the conductor and shouted, "Why didn't you get me up? I missed my stop. I missed my stop!" Then, for the next ten minutes, he stood there bawling him out. Finally, he turned around and left.

One of the passengers who had seen the whole thing said to conductor, "Did you ever see a madder man in all your life?"

"Yeah, I saw one," he answered.

"Who was that?"

"That was the man I put off the train at 6:30 this morning."

8.

A man sat by a window on the bus and kept spitting out, saying, ——(spit, spit, spit) "What a driver, what a driver!"

Finally, the driver of the bus could stand it no longer. He stopped the bus, stormed back to where the man was and said, "If you don't like the way I drive this bus you can get off! Right now!"

The man answered, "Oh, no, no. I wasn't talking about you. Let me explain."

"You see, I work back there in that parking lot and today we had just filled the lot with cars when the ugliest woman I've ever seen came in driving the biggest Lincoln I've ever seen. I said to her, "Sorry mam, but you're too late. We just filled up the lot."

She looked around and saw a space across the way and said, "There's a place right over there."

I answered, "No mam, that place isn't big enough for this car. You can't get it in there."

She said, "Sure you can. Go ahead. Put it there," and she kept insisting.

Finally I said, "Lady, nobody can put a big car like this into a space that small."

She wrinkled up her ugly face in a big grin and said, "I'll bet you a big, fat kiss I could."

The passenger turned toward the bus window again and said, ——- (spit, spit, spit), "What a driver, what a driver!"

9.

Some tourists were visiting the southwestern U.S. and went out to an Indian village in Arizona. Their guide said, "Would you like to meet an Indian with a remarkable memory? He never forgets anything."

"Sure," they answered.

He took them over to an old man seated on the ground draped in his blanket and said, "There he is."

The guide said, "How!" and the old Indian looked up and answered, "How!"

"Ask him any question you want to," said the guide.

The tourist thought for a moment and asked, "What did you have for breakfast on the third Thursday of July, 1983?"

The old Indian looked up and without hesitation answered, "Eggs."

The tourist was amazed. He couldn't get over it. When they arrived back home he told his friends of the trip and the Indian with the amazing memory. One of the men answered, "That doesn't sound so great. He probably had eggs for breakfast every day."

"I didn't think of that," said the man. "You're probably right."

Ten years later the same tourist was back visiting the reservation. The guide said, "Do you want to see an Indian with a remarkable memory? He never forgets anything."

"Oh yeah," said the skeptical tourist, as he thought of the eggs. "I don't believe it. Let me see him."

The guide took him over and the tourist walked up to him and said, "How!"

The old Indian looked up, thought for a moment and then answered,————————- "Scrambled."

10.

A man and his wife went to Hawaii.

As soon as they left the airplane, they found a Hawaiian and the man asked,

"Are you Hawaiian?"

"Yes," he answered.

"Well, my wife and I have been arguing for the last ten years about how you pronounce this place. She says Hawaii and I say Havaii. Which is right?"

"Havaii," he answered.

"Ah, "said the man. "that proves I'm right. Thank you very much."

"You're velcome," he answered.

11.

A man arrived too late to get his plane and had to wait another two hours. While he was waiting he was looking around the airport. He saw some scales with a sign that said, "Your Weight and Your Future for a Quarter."

He stepped on the scales and dropped in a quarter and out came a card that read, "You are a white man —— weight 179 pounds ——and are on your way to Baltimore."

"Wow, that's great!" he said.

Later he came by the scales again and there was an Indian with a blanket around him and a feathered headdress on. He stepped on the scales and out came a card. He read it but before he could walk away the man asked, "Can I read your card?"

"Ug," answered the Indian and handed him the card.

The man read, "You are an Indian—— weight 183 pounds ——and are on your way to Phoenix."

"Is that right?" asked the man. Again the Indian answered, "Ug."

The man went over and sat down and thought about it. He decided that there must be someone who was hiding and watching the scales and typing out the cards.

So he went looking for the Indian, found him and asked if he could rent the blanket and headdress. The Indian agreed and the man went back to the scales. He hid around the corner until he had put on the blanket and headdress and then ran around and jumped on the scales.

Out came a card which said, "You are still a white man and weigh 179 pounds and while you were fooling around on these scales you missed your plane to Baltimore."

12.

Two guys went on a trip to see the mountains of the west.

They had traveled across the plains for hours and at the end of the day they finally saw the mountains. But, before they drove into them, they decided to stop overnight and explore them the next day.

The next morning one of them said, "I can't wait. It's only a couple of blocks over to the mountains. I'm gonna walk over and look around. I'll be back in a little while."

The other answered, "That's fine. I'll eat breakfast and wait for you here."

The mountains, that looked so close, proved to be 10 miles away and the guy walked and walked and walked.

Meanwhile, the other guy finished breakfast and sat down to wait. After waiting all morning and most of the afternoon, he started the car and went looking for the other guy.

Finally, he found him and pulled off the road. He walked over to the side and there in a little valley he could see him as he was starting to wade across a little stream with his shoes off and his pants rolled up high.

He hollered down to him, "You don't have to take off your shoes and roll up your pants to cross that little stream. It's only about two feet wide."

The other hollered back, "I'm not taking any chances. I don't intend to be fooled twice in the same day."

13.

"Would you like a ride to town?" said the man to the young hitchhiker.

"Sure would," he answered.

"Well, before we get going I need to check the turn signals on my car. Would you get out in front and tell me if they are working?"

"Yep," he answered and went to the front of the car.

The man turned on the signals and the young guy hollered,

"yes————-no————-yes————-no————-yes—————no"

14.

Jose (Ho-say) was from Mexico and came to visit in the United States. He saw all the sights and went home. When he gathered his friends to tell them about his trip, Jose described the big football game."

"What a game! What a game! I never saw anything so exciting in my whole life. There must have been 60,000 people there. And these people, they are all so friendly!

"I was sitting way up in the balcony by the flags and before the game began all of the people stood and looked up at me and sang, 'Hose can you see?'"

15.

An Englishman came to visit the United States. He saw the sights in many states and was finishing his trip in New York City. As he was riding in a cab looking around the city the driver said, "So, you're from England. How would you like to hear some American humor?"

"Oh, by all means, my good man," answered the Englishman.

"Well, let me give you a riddle. My father and my mother had a baby. It wasn't my brother and it wasn't my sister. Who was it?"

The Englishman thought a minute and then answered, "But I say. I don't know."

The cab driver answered, "It was me! Ha, Ha, Ha."

The Englishman thought that was funny and returned to England with that riddle in mind. He called a party for his friends to tell them of his experiences in America. While they were there he asked, "Would you like to hear some American humor?"

They answered , "By all means."

"Let me give you a riddle," he said. "My father and my mother had a baby. It wasn't my sister and it wasn't my brother. Who was it?" They sat thinking for a minute and then gave up.

He smiled and answered, "It was a taxi cab driver in New York City."

16.

A police officer pulled a guy over for speeding and said:

"You were going way too fast! May I see your driver's license?"

The driver said, "But I wasn't going fast."

"Yes you were," replied the officer. "Let's see your license."

The driver paused for a moment and then replied, "I don't have one. They took it away after my fifth DWI."

"Really?" said the officer, "Well let me check your owner's card."

"Oh, this isn't my car."

"Whose is it?"

"Some woman. I just stole it about ten minutes ago."

"You stole it?'

"Yeah, but come to think of it, I saw the owner's card in the glove
compartment when I put my gun in there."

"There's a gun in the glove box?"

"Yeah, the one I shot the woman with."

"What woman?"

The one who owns the car. The same one whose body I put in the trunk."

"In this car?"

"Yes sir."

"Just a minute. Don't move. Keep your hands on the steering wheel."

The officer immediately called his captain on the radio. The car was

quickly surrounded by police and the captain approached the driver

with great caution.

"Mister, you don't have a license?"

"Oh, yes sir, here it is," and he handed it to the captain.

"Whose car is this?" asked the captain.

"It's mine, sir," he said as he handed the captain his owner's card.

"Would you slowly open your glove box so I can see if it has a gun in it?"

"Yes, sir, but there's no gun in it." He opened the glove box and it was empty.

"All right, all right. Let's open the trunk. I have been told there is a body in it."

"No problem," said the driver and he opened the trunk and it was empty.

The captain was amazed. "I don't understand it. The officer who stopped you said you didn't have a license, had stolen the car, had a gun in the glove box and a dead body in the trunk."

"Yeah," answered the driver, " and I'll bet he told you I was speeding too."

18.

As a senior citizen was driving down the freeway, his car phone rang.

Answering, he heard his wife's voice urgently warning him, "Herman, I just heard on the news that there's a car going the wrong way on Interstate 77. Please be careful!"

"You're right ," said Herman, "I'm on Interstate 77 and it's not just one car going the wrong way. It's hundreds of them!"

19.

Two elderly women were out driving in a large car—both could barely see over the dashboard. As they were cruising along, they came to an intersection. The stoplight was red, but they just went on through.

The woman in the passenger seat thought to herself 'I must be losing it. I could have sworn we just went through a red light.' After a few more minutes, they came to another intersection and the light was red. Again, they went right through. The woman in the passenger seat was almost sure that the light had been red but was really concerned that she was losing it. She was getting nervous.

At the next intersection, sure enough, the light was red and they went on through. So, she turned to the other woman and said, "Mildred, did you know that we just ran through three red lights in a row? You could have killed us both!"

Mildred turned to her and said, "Good Heavens, am I driving?"

20.

Sherlock Holmes and Dr. Watson go on a camping trip, and after finishing their dinner they go to their tent, lay down on their cots and go to sleep.

Some hours later, Holmes wakes up and calls out to his faithful friend. "Watson, look up at the sky and tell me what you see."

"I see millions and millions of stars, Holmes" exclaims Watson.

"That's right," says Holmes, "And what do you deduce from that?"

Watson ponders for a minute. "Well, astronomically, it tells me that there are millions of galaxies and potentially billions of planets. Astrologically, I observe that Saturn is in Leo. Horologically, I deduce that the time is approximately a quarter past three. Meteorologically, I suspect that we will have a beautiful day tomorrow. Theologically, I can see that God is all powerful, and that we are a small and insignificant part of the universe. And now, Holmes, what do you deduce from seeing the stars.?"

"Watson, you idiot!" exclaims Holmes, "I deduce that somebody's stolen our tent!"

WORK

1.

Arthur went to work for the highway department. They put him on the crew painting lines down the middle of the road.

The first day he came in and they asked how much he had painted. "Three miles," he answered with a happy expression. They congratulated him.

The next day they asked how much and he answered, "One-half mile," and he didn't look very happy.

The third day they asked and he said, "Two hundred feet."

"Look," they said, "how could you start with three miles and in two days drop down to two hundred feet?"

"Well," he answered with anger, "What do you expect? I keep getting farther and farther away from the paint bucket!"

2.

Two men were painting a house.

One of them was up on a ladder when the other came over and grabbing the ladder said, "Do you have a good hold on that paint brush?"

"Yeah," answered the other, "Why?"

"Cause I'm going to move the ladder," he said.

3.

A landscape architect was the boss on a new project. He was in his office when a salesman came by to present a new product.

Work

Every few minutes the boss would walk over to the window and holler,

"Green side up."

After a few times doing this the salesman asked him what that meant.

"Well," he explained, "I hired an Aggie this morning and put him out there planting grass."

4.

The young man was hired to work for the blacksmith, but it didn't work out very well. It happened this way. The young man was on the job the first day and the blacksmith said, "Pick up those tongs over there."

"Yeah, yeah," he answered.

"Now, go get that horseshoe off the fire and put it on the anvil."

"Yeah, yeah," he answered.

"Now, when I nod my head, you hit it with the hammer."

With a question on his face the young man looked at the blacksmith's head. "Yeah, yeah," he answered.

Right after that the blacksmith was seen chasing him out of town.

5.

A man wanted to cut wood for his fireplace so he went to a rental company to rent a chain saw.

He brought it back after the first day and said that it didn't work very well. He was only able to cut about a half a cord of wood even though he worked all day on it.

The manager told him that he could have it free of charge for another day and that he must have had some trouble getting use to it.

The man brought it back after the next day saying it still didn't work well and that he only cut about one-third of a cord that day.

The manager said he wanted to take a look at it. "Come with me," he said and took the man over to a big pile of logs.

He laid one aside to cut it and then pulled the rope to start the saw. The engine started up and the customer jumped back and hollered, "What's that noise? What's that noise?"

6.

Two young guys who weren't very smart went to work on a road crew and had the job of digging a big hole. It was the hot summer time.

They were down in the hole when one of them stopped and wiped the sweat from his face.

"Hey, I was just thinking," he said, How come me and you are sweatin' it out in this big, hot hole when the boss just sits up there in that air conditioned trailer, drinking coolade and eatin' doughnuts?"

"I been wonderin' the same thing," answered the other. "Why don't you go and ask him?

"I think I will," he answered and climbed out of the hole.

He went over to the shack, walked in and said, "Hey, boss, me and this other guy wanna know somethin."

"What is it?" asked the boss.

"Well, how come me and him are out there in that hole on this hot day doing all the heavy work and you're sittin' in this air conditioned shack drinkin' coolade and eatin' doughnuts?"

"Oh, we call that strategy." .

"Strategy? What's that?"

"Come out here and let me demonstrate, he answered as he walked out.

He lifted his hand up in front of a big tree trunk and said, "Now, when I count to three, you hit my hand as hard as you can."

He started counting "One—-two—-three." But just before three, he moved his hand and the young man swung and hit the tree.—- Smack!

"Ohhhhhhh, Ohhhhhhhhhhh." shouted the young guy as he jumped up and down, rubbing his hand.

"Now that's strategy," said the boss and he went back inside the trailer.

The young guy went back to the hole still rubbing his hand as he climbed down. The other guy asked, "What did he say? What did he say?"

"Well, he told me it was just a matter of strategy."

"Strategy, what's that?"

"Well, step over here and I'll show you," he answered.

Since there wasn't any tree he put his hand up in front of his face and said, "Now, when I count to three, you hit my hand."

7.

A blacksmith was making horseshoes . He took one from the furnace and, using the tongs, put it on the anvil.

A young guy from the city came strutting in. He acted like he knew it all and was bragging about what he had learned since he had gone to the big city.

As he was talking he reached over and picked up the horseshoe, but then he dropped it fast and stuck his hand in his pocket.

"Kinda hot?" asked the blacksmith with a smile.

"No," answered the young guy, "It just doesn't take me long to look at a horseshoe."

8.

A handyman went through the neighborhood knocking on doors. "Need any help? I'm a handyman," he said to one lady.

"We might," she answered. "Check with my husband. He's around back."

He walked around to the back and there was the husband working in the garage. "Need any help? I'm a handyman and can mow yards, repair fences or whatever," he said.

"Well, you came at the right time. I need some painting done. Do you do that kind of work?"

"Yep, I'm a painter , the world's best. What do yuh need painting?"

"Well, I need the porch painted around in front. It's pretty big but you may be able to get it painted in one day. Here's the bucket of paint and the brush. You can get started right now."

"OK, I'll get right to it," he answered as he picked up the bucket and the brush and headed around to the front. He was only gone a couple of hours when he came back. "What do you need?" said the man in the garage.

"Well, I'm all through."

"How could you be? That is a huge porch!"

"Aw, it ain't all that big. And besides it ain't a Porsch; it's a Mercedes!"

APPENDIX
Additional Selections

1.

Stress Dieting

A Diet Designed To Cope With Stress

Feeling Good? No problem!

Breakfast
  1 Grapefruit
  1 Slice whole wheat toast
  8 Ounces Skim Milk
Lunch
  4 Ounces Leaned Broiled Chicken Breast
  1 Cup Steamed Spinach
  1 Cup Herbal Tea
  1 Oreo Cookie
Stress Attack? —- You Need Help!
Midafternoon Snack
  Rest of Oreos in Package
  2 Pints of Rocky Road Ice Cream
1 Jar Hot Fudge Sauce, Nuts, Cherries, Whipped Cream
Dinner
  2 Loaves Garlic Bread With Cheese
  1 Large Sausage/Mushroom/Pepperoni/ Cheese Pizza

1 Milky Way or Snickers Candy Bar
     Stress Signals Again?
     Late Night News -
1 Whole Frozen Cheesecake Eaten Directly from Box

Stress Gone?—-A Successful Day! Sleep Well!

2.

Calorie Counting for Stress Dieting

1. If you eat something without anyone seeing you eat it, it has no calories.

2. When you eat with someone else, if you eat less than they do, calories don't count.

3. If you drink a diet soda with a dessert, the calories in the dessert are canceled out by the diet soda.

4. Calories in Video related foods — such as Milk Duds, Buttered Popcorn, Junior Mints, Red Hots and Tootsie Rolls -are part of the entire Entertainment Package and not part of one's personal diet so they are never counted.

5. The process of breakage causes calorie leakage. Therefore, cookie pieces contain no calories!

6. Additionally, and this is important, calories are not formed in cookies until the baking process is in effect. If you eat cookie dough, you can deduct the equivalent number of calories it would have been if the cookies had been baked.

7. Important footnote! If you go ahead and eat the whole batch of dough without baking a single cookie, you receive an additional bonus of 100 deducted calories for your dedication in preventing calorie consumption.

3.

Does Exercise Help?

1. It is well documented that for every mile you jog, you add one minute to your life. This enables you, at age 85, to spend $5,000 per month for an additional five months in a nursing home.

2. My grandmother started walking five miles a day when she was sixty. She is now 97 and we don't know where she is.

3. I joined a health club last year to lose weight and spent about $400. Haven't lost a pound. Apparently you have to attend the health club regularly.

4. I have to exercise early in the morning before my brain figures out what I am doing.

5. I don't exercise at all. If God meant for us to touch our toes, he would have put them further up on our body.

6. I like long walks away from my home, especially when they are taken by people who annoy me.

7. I have flabby thighs, but fortunately my stomach covers them.

8. If you are going to try cross country skiing, start with a small country.

9. The advantage of exercising every day is that you die healthier.

4.

Reward for Lost Dog

DESCRIPTION:

THREE LEGS
    BLIND IN LEFT EYE
    TAIL BROKEN
    MISSING RIGHT EAR

ANSWERS TO NAME OF "LUCKY"

5.

Garage

Labor Rates

Regular charges	24.50
If you wait	30.00
If you watch	35.00
If you help	50.00
If you worked on it yourself	60.00
If you laugh	75.00

6.

How to Raise Money for Projects

(With threats of the athletic program being curtailed the Athletic Director reports to the Committee on Priorities at the University). It has been suggested that we shut down our football program but I have good news. I just figured out a way we can get the money we need without having to do this.

For some time I have considered investing in a large cat ranch between Greer and Greenville just off highway 29. It is my purpose to start rather small with about one million cats.

Each cat averages about twelve kittens a year and the skins can be sold for about twenty cents for the white ones and up to forty cents for the black ones. (Now you cat lovers just chill out for a minute).

This will give us twelve million cat skins to sell on an average price of around thirty-two cents making our revenue about three million dollars a year. This actually averages out to about ten thousand dollars a day excluding Sundays and holidays.

A good upper Piedmont cat man can skin about fifty cats per day at a wage of three dollars fifteen cents an hour. It will take only 663 men to operate the ranch so the net profit will be over eight thousand two hundred a day.

The cats will be fed on rats exclusively. Rats multiply four times as fast as cats so we would start a rat farm adjacent to our cat ranch.

If we start with a million rats we will have four rats per cat per day. The rats will be fed on the carcasses of the cats we've skinned. This will give each rat a quarter of a cat.

You can see by this that the business is a clean operation, self supporting, and has truly automatic routes. The cats will eat the rats, the rats will eat the cats and we will get the skins.

Eventually it is my hope to cross the cats with snakes so they will skin themselves twice a year. This would save the labor costs for skinning as well as give us two skins for one cat.

I'm going to go pretty heavy in this deal and hope that the money we make will enable us to pursue some of the projects we have selected so that we might continue to be a great university.

7.

How to Know You're Growing Older

1 Everything hurts and what doesn't hurt doesn't work.

2 You feel like the morning after but you haven't been anywhere.

3 Your little black book contains only names ending in M.D.

4 You get winded playing chess.

5 You get worn out dialing long distance.

6   You finally reach the top of the ladder only to find it leaning against the wrong wall.

7   You join a health club and don't go.

8   You know all the answers but nobody asks you the questions.

9   You look forward to a dull evening.

10 You sit in a rocking chair but can't get it going.

11 You knees buckle but your belt won't.

12 You're 17 around the neck, 44 around the waist and 110 around the golf course.

13 Your back goes out more often than you do.

14 The only exercise you get is in attending the funerals of your friends who exercise.

15 You've got too much room in the house but not enough room in the medicine cabinet.

16 You sink your teeth into a steak and they stay there.

17 You can't read all these things because the print's too small.

8.

Bumper Stickers

1. I used to have a handle on life but it broke.

2. You're just jealous because the voices only talk to ME.

3. All men are idiots and I married their king.

4. IRS —- We've got what it takes to take what you've got.

5. Hard work has a future pay off. Laziness pays off now.

6. Out of my mind. . ..Back in five minutes..

7. Your kid may be an honor student but you're still an idiot.

8. I took an IQ test and the results were negative.

9. Where there's a will . . .. I want to be in it.

10. It's lonely at the top but you eat better up there.

11. Consciousness: That annoying time between naps.

12. Ever stop to think, and forget to start again?

13. Taxation WITH representation ain't so hot either.

14. My wife keeps complaining that I never listen to her . . . or something like that.

9.

What Mama Taught Me

1. She taught me there's a time and place for everything - "I just finished cleaning the house. If you are going to kill each other, do it outside."

2. She taught me religion - "You had better pray that the stuff you spilled will come out of the carpet."

3. She taught me logic - "Because I said so, that's why."

4. She taught me foresight - "Make sure you wear clean underwear. You never know when you might be in an accident and be taken to a hospital."

5. She taught me control - "You keep on laughing and I will give you something to cry about."

6. She taught me osmosis - "Shut your mouth and eat your supper."

7. She taught me how to be a contortionist - "Look at the back of your neck. It's filthy."

8. She taught me about stamina - "You sit there until all that spinach is gone."

9. She taught me about weather - "Your room looks like it was hit by a tornado."

10. She taught me to keep count - "If I told you once, I told you a million times, don't exaggerate."

11. She taught me self control -" I made that cake for my bridge club. Don't you go near it."

12. She taught me behavior modification -"Stop acting like your father."

10.

Famous Last Words

1. I bet I'll get a world record for this.

2. He's probably just hibernating.

3. I wonder where the mother bear is.

4. Just pull the pin and count to what?

5. The odds of that happening are a million to one.

6. Are you sure the power is off?

7. I'll hold it while you light the fuse

8. Which wire am I suppose to cut?

9. I've seen this done on TV.

10. These are the good kind of mushrooms.

11. You look just like Charles Manson.

12. I hope they speak English.

13. It's strong enough for both of us.

14. You wouldn't hit a guy with glasses on.

15. Nice doggie.

16. Hey, that's not a violin in that case.

17. Watch me, I can do this with my eyes closed.

11.

Music in The Church

An old farmer went to the city one weekend and attended the big church.

He came home and his wife asked him how it was. "Well," said the farmer, 'it was good. They did something different, however; they sang praise choruses instead of regular songs."

"Praise choruses," said his wife. "What are those?'

"Well," he answered, "it's like this. If I were to say to you, 'Martha, the cows are in the corn.' that would be a hymn. But if I were to say,

> 'Martha, Martha, Martha,
> Oh, Martha, Martha, Martha,
> the cows, the big cows, the brown cows, the white cows,
> the cows, cows, cows
> are in the corn,
> in the corn
> in the corn
> the corn, corn, corn'

And were to repeat the whole thing two or three times, that would be a praise chorus."

On the exact same Sunday, a young Christian from the city went out to the country and attended a small church. He came home and his wife asked him how it was.

"Well," said the young man, "it was pretty cool. But they did something different. They sang hymns instead of regular songs."

"Hymns," said his wife, "what are those?"

"It's like this," he said. " If I were to say to you, 'Martha, the cows are in the corn' that would be a regular song. But if I were to say,

'Oh, Martha, dear Martha, hear thou my cry,
Turn thy whole wondrous ear by and by.

For the way of the animals, who can explain
Hearkenest they not in God's sun or his rain.

They have torn free from shackles, their warm pens eschewed
And all my sweet corn they have eagerly chewed.'

Then, if I do only verse one, two and four with a key change on the last verse, that would be a hymn."

12.

Fitting Everybody into One Mold

I read the story that a bunch of animals decided to do something to meet the problems of the world. So they started a school.

The school adopted a curriculum of running, climbing, swimming and flying. Everyone enrolled was required to take all four subjects.

There were four enrolled: a duck, a rabbit, a squirrel and an eagle.

The duck was excellent in swimming, in fact, better than the instructor. But he only made passing grades in flying and was very poor in running. This caused his web feet to get blisters so he became only average in swimming. But average was better than anyone else so nobody worried about it, except the duck.

The rabbit started at the top of his class in running, but developed a nervous twitch in his leg muscles because of so much make up work in swimming.

The squirrel was excellent in climbing but was constantly frustrated in flying class because his teacher made him start from the ground up instead of from the treetop down. He developed "charlie horses" from overexertion and so only got a C in climbing and a D in running.

The eagle was a problem child and was severely disciplined for not cooperating. In climbing classes he was first to the top of the tree but insisted on flying to get there.

All in all the school was a flop.

13.

And God populated the earth with broccoli and cauliflower and spinach, green and yellow vegetables of all kinds, so man and woman would live long and healthy lives.

And Satan brought forth McDonald's with the 99 cent double cheeseburger. And Satan said to man, 'You want fries with that?" And man said, 'Supersize them." And man gained pounds.

And God created the healthful yogurt, that woman might keep her figure. And Satan brought forth chocolate. And woman gained pounds.

And God said, "Try my crispy fresh salad." And Satan brought forth ice cream. And woman gained many pounds.

And God said, " I have sent you heart-healthy vegetables and olive oil with which to cook them." And Satan brought forth chicken fried steak so big it needed its own platter. And man gained many pounds and his cholesterol went through the roof.

And God brought forth running shoes and man resolved to lose those extra pounds. And Satan brought forth cable TV with remote control so man would not have to toil to change channels. And man gained many more pounds.

And God brought forth the potato, a vegetable naturally low in fat and brimming with nutrition. And Satan peeled off the healthful skin and sliced the starchy center into chips and deep fried them. And he made sour cream dip also.

And man clutched his remote control and ate the potato chips swaddled in cholesterol. And Satan saw and said, "It is good."

And man went into cardiac arrest. And God sighed and created quadruple bypass surgery.

And Satan made HMO's but they didn't work, so he just gave up.

14.

Wisdom in Everyday clothes!

1. My husband and I argued over religious differences.
   He thought he was God and I didn't agree.

2. I don't suffer from insanity; I enjoy every minute of it.

3. Some people are alive only because it's illegal to kill them.

4. I used to have a handle on life, but it broke. . .

5. You're just jealous because the voices only talk to me

6. I'm not a complete idiot — Some parts are still missing.

7. Consciousness: That annoying time between naps.

8. Being 'over the hill' is much better than being under it!

9. Wrinkled Was Not One of the Things I Wanted to Be When I Grew up.

10. Did you say, "Go back to college?" I already Have a College Degree. Do You Want Fries With your order?

11. He who dies with the most toys is nonetheless DEAD.

12. Eggs. . .A day's work for a chicken. Ham . . . a lifetime commitment for a pig.

13. The original point and click was a Smith & Wesson pistol.

14. Be a Procastinater — Do it Now!

Index

Capitalized words indicate subject headings in book

Index

Index

Index

Index

Index

Index